CONTENTS

INTERVENTIONS AND SOCIAL STRATEGIES

INTERNATIONAL PERSPECTIVES

FOREWORD & ACKNOWLEDGEMENTS

We are pleased to be able to publish some of the contributions to ISTD's 1996 annual residential conference. A wide range of practitioners and academics from both this country and abroad joined us at Keele University for this event. We have provided transcripts of those plenary contributions where speakers were unable to supply texts: readers will notice that some of the following were written to be heard rather than read. Where workshop leaders were kind enough to supply us with copies of reports of, or papers written for, their sessions, we have included them, although we have edited some contributions, on the grounds of space. Papers are not necessarily grouped as they were on the programme, but are divided into broad sections, by topic.

Other seminar contributions came from: Arne Andresen, Project Co-ordinator, Council of Europe, Pompidou Group Drug Reduction Staff Training Programme • Guy Gardener, Superintendent, Kent County Constabulary • Teresa Jankowska, Team Leader, Healthy Options Team • Maggy Lee and Jane Mounteney, Researchers, Institute for the Study of Drug Dependence • Maciej Lubik, World Customs Organisation Regional Intelligence Liaison Office • Frank McGoldrick, Co-ordinator, Research Group on Chemical Dependency, Belfast • Jesse Morgan, Lincoln Hospital, New York • Katalin Szomor, Hungarian Inter-ministerial Drug Committee.

Particular thanks go to all our speakers and workshop leaders, to Professor Michael Hough, who took the chair at the conference at short notice when Andrew Coyle found himself unavoidably detained at Brixton Prison, and to the hard-working conference team - Carol Martin, Stephanie Hayman, Julie Grogan, Nina Cope, Nic Groombridge, Kathy Biggar and Bill Baker. We were most grateful to the Prison Service and the Home Office for financial support and to Keele University for their hospitality and efficiency. Particular thanks, also to Stephanie Hayman and Sue McCormick for their help with early drafts of this report, to Amberwood Graphics for their patience with the transcription and production work, and to Stewart Harkness for the cover photo. Responsibility for the final product rests with me.

Julia Braggins
Director, ISTD

March 1997

INTRODUCTION

The 'Tackling Drugs Together' initiative is unusual in the contemporary political landscape for the extent to which it has managed to command consensus. When the White Paper was published in 1995, it was widely welcomed for marking out a sensible approach to a difficult and complex set of problems. Though it was not without its critics, there was widespread appreciation of the emphasis it placed on tackling drug problems rather than winning votes.

This report represents the proceedings of the 1996 ISTD annual residential conference, 'Tackling Drugs Together: One Year On'. It seemed timely then to take stock of the initiative; and although some time has elapsed since then, the topic seems no less important or timely today. At the time of the conference, it was abundantly clear - as these papers show - that the DAT/DRG structures were starting to achieve something, and that the initiative was yielding some benefits. There was a greatly increased level of contact and mutual understanding between different agencies involved in dealing with drug issues, and much greater visibility and priority for drug issues. No-one doubts that DATs and DRGs have made a very promising start in partnership work.

The real challenge lies ahead, of course, in ensuring that the partnership structures deliver tangible improvements in provision. These papers point to some of the obstacles which have to be overcome. The first, as ever, is resources. Effective partnership can yield economies at the margin, but inter-agency committees cannot *substitute* for resources. With continued downward pressure on public spending, and intense competition for cash within health criminal justice and education, the prospect for resourcing drug services properly must be uncertain.

Secondly, work must be done to make sure that DATs and DRGs - and whatever in time replaces them - mesh properly with other partnership structures - especially those which oversee the resourcing of community care and those which address community safety.

Finally, DATs and DRGs have a critical role to play in mediating between the political pressures for action which has the *appearance* of firm and decisive action - talking tough on drugs - and the reality that the social harms caused by problem drug use are often tackled most effectively though a - politically unattractive - low-key pragmatism. If the 'Tackling Drugs Together' initiative helps to bring about a more open and honest climate of public debate on drugs, this will have been a significant achievement.

Professor Michael Hough
Criminal Policy Research Unit, South Bank University

TACKLING DRUGS TOGETHER - AN OVERVIEW

Stephen Rimmer, Director of the
Central Drugs Co-ordination Unit

It may not seem terribly exciting to say so, but this strategy represented a fairly fundamental shift in government thinking. The CDCU was set up in January 1994 by the Prime Minister, originally just to devise what ended up as being a Green Paper and then a White Paper but we managed to continue to function. We are in a way an expression of government failure, in the sense that most difficult policy issues do not fit easily within the monolithic blocks of central government departments. Drugs is clearly by no means the only issue of this kind.

We are very small, there are six of us in total. We are a tiny bit of central government, which gives us a lot of freedom. I and my colleagues can do things in a more external, 'independent' way than the big government departments. But it also means that when big questions come into play, particularly about resources, we have to try and secure consensus amongst our colleagues and that can prove difficult. And our only real clout is that we report direct to Tony Newton, otherwise known as the Lord President, who is the chair of the Cabinet Sub-Committee on Drugs and has overall responsibility for its implementation. Tony Newton has been in on the Drugs Strategy since the start, he understands it from back to front. He is very committed to its effective implementation and he has a very effective way of dealing with his colleagues.

The White Paper is deliberately focused on very specific tasks, clear bits of work that have to be done within given time scales. That led to the criticism that this is just a management framework, it isn't underpinned by a coherent philosophy. But I think in fact it tries to get the best of both worlds in terms of setting out an overall statement of purpose and then developing tasks within that framework. And that relates to local action as well as national action. This is a very interesting aspect of this strategy. It is still pretty new for this country and in most European countries, or the ones I have spoken to, that is the element of what we are doing that is particularly of interest: the attempt to marry up or reconcile, if reconcile is the word, central government objectives with local agendas and local action. I would like to think the strategy is genuinely consultative and focused and consensus building. Clearly it starts to fail the minute it gets tossed around like a political football.

What do I think has been achieved in the first year? Political consensus: that can be criticised. It can be seen as demonstrating the cloying nature of the subject that people aren't allowed to make thought-provoking/provocative statements. But I think from my perspective, it is helpful to know that an election is unlikely to change the framework or the strategy very much. It is helpful to know that the policy is not only, or primarily being driven by short-term political gains. Again in most areas of social policy, that cannot be taken for granted, it has to be worked at. What has helped that particularly in our case, is that Tony Newton deals with the subject on a very inclusive participatory basis. He does listen to people who know what they are talking about, and he has worked very hard to sustain that consensus.

The tasks for 95-96 were achieved on time. Most of those were processes - strategies being developed, commitments being fulfilled in terms of resources. But it is important to sustain the momentum so that those boxes get ticked. I think I am right in saying that by now all the police strategies have been published in England; some of them got a lot of attention - Operation Jigsaw for the Greater Manchester Police, while the Metropolitan Police have Operation Crackdown. They have all been quite impressive, in my view. The Prison Service have done particularly well in developing strategies locally over the past 12 months. The simple fact, for example, that MDT got implemented without significant control problems is an achievement in terms of the professionalism of the staff involved. All schools have got the materials from the DFEE in terms of guidance in respect of drug-related incidents, and OFSTED are now checking the extent to which those are being implemented and I think that the initial views of OFSTED are going to prove quite favourable. Another key area is pubs/clubs/raves etc. Young people are always very interesting to the media. The Home Office put guidance out to local authorities and others a couple of months ago, and that should be going out in its final version soon. Again I think it exemplifies a highly commendable, balanced approach in terms of focusing on targeting drugs supplies into clubs, providing information, education, training, and also safety measures.

On the treatment side I think the most significant development has been the publication of the

Effectiveness Review which came out at the beginning of May, and not just for generating an extra £6 million for particular programmes which are now going through Health Authorities. It is a monumentally rational, objective, empirical, piece of work from a task force which looked at any piece of evidence with a properly sceptical eye and came up with only those conclusions that it felt the evidence merited.

We do now have some baseline information which we have never really had nationally before. This does give some flavour of what is happening in terms of trends. Some of the performance indicators are more flawed than others - I think the police KPI which focuses on arrests under the '71 Act is particularly vague - but they give us some sense of progress over time, which we have not had before on a national basis. Certainly in the last twelve months, the level of concern amongst the public, via the media and also directly, I think, has been significant. There have been particular points at which that has come to fruition and there is no question that the death of Lean Betts hit the consciousness of an awful lot of people. Her parents have taken their grief and anger forward in terms of providing information and ideas to help parents particularly to come to terms with the reality of drugs and what may or may not help their children, and I think that has been very positive and very helpful. We have also just had published the British Crime Survey and Health Education Authority Survey results. As with any major survey, you can take many inferences from them, but a lot of the findings help to reduce some of the media hysteria about drugs and young people which is good.

At local level the focus has been on the Drug Action Teams. The Action Plans which DATs have produced have been very good; they have exceeded our expectations. I certainly hope that we got some useful material out of them for the digest which went to DATs and others in April. Of course there is variety: some DATs have just been taken from existing inter-agency groups, others genuinely started from scratch. We went to all of them last Autumn and it was quite clear that we would not all be moving at the same pace. There have also been a lot of issues about getting local community consultation networks, the Drugs Reference Groups and others set up through the DATs and that is a complicated, difficult and sometimes sensitive process. DATs need time to develop their relationships effectively at a local level and if they don't do that they will be a waste of time.

That is the summary: the information needs to be clarified. We are just sending out some useful work done by the ISDD, which should help a lot of the DATs gain a bit more confidence in dealing with the complexities of the information: which bits matter, which bits they can, frankly, leave to one side, which bits they should have a look at, which bits they haven't got. But there are unquestionably difficult decisions yet to be taken and I think the key for a lot of DATs will come when they start to talk seriously about the resources they have got, collectively and individually, the priorities they have signed up to, and the inevitable (and it will be inevitable), lack of congruence between the two in certain areas.

Last month we had a commemorative 'one year on' event which the Prime Minister led. It was quite interesting to see the reaction to that, but particularly to the Parents' Guide which quite a lot of you will have seen: it got subject to a moral crusade, if that is the phrase, from some of the papers. Again the emphasis had been to try and get a balanced approach from clear information that presented, in an objective way, information about drugs including the consequences of using them. It got castigated in some quarters for in effect not being sufficiently judgemental. In fact the take-up rate has been excellent: 150,000 have already gone out to individual parents at their request and I think the HEA are doing another print run of half a million. But despite the fact that I think this is a balanced strategy, it clearly doesn't satisfy everyone.

We have just appointed a senior international drugs coordinator which sounds pretty exciting - that person will be responsible from the 1st July for coordinating the UK's efforts overseas in the context of drugs enforcement. And we also announced the details of a £2 million challenge fund which is entirely new money in drugs terms. It is a competitive fund as all these things have to be, but it is an opportunity at about the right time for a lot of DATs to work collectively towards a particular common goal. DATs must add value; there is not a lot of point meeting every three months and just chatting about things.

So that is the basic theme: to keep the momentum going, to focus on the partnership, and to broaden out the constituency as far as possible. The White Paper got alot of credit at professional and political level but it did not impinge on public consciousness. I think we need to keep raising the profile of what the strategy is trying to achieve and how best people can help that, as we move forward.

Finally and briefly, some thoughts about the future. The resources issue dominates as always. There is never enough to do everything, nor even half of everything you want to do. Certainly there is a general perception that by no means all the resources that are currently invested (we are talking about over half a billion pounds a year and that is just through the statutory agencies) are being used as coherently and practically as one would like. One specific area, a very important issue at the moment, is drugs services in prisons. As most of you will know, that is a pretty chaotic picture at present. It depends on particular arrangements in particular areas as to what goes on or indeed what doesn't and we are trying to pull that together so that there is a clearly understood framework within which services can be provided both while prisoners are in custody and then when they are released back to their neighbourhoods. The complicated set of interactions that that entails needs clarifying as do the resources that are available for it.

There is a lot spoken about joint commissioning: clearly some agencies, health and local authorities are used to doing it in this field as in others. But there doesn't seem to be a particular momentum generated in a lot of DATs to look at pooling resources, for all sorts of understandable reasons. Having worked in a multi agency forum myself, I know that some of those difficulties require time and patience as much as ideas or best practice from elsewhere.

Evaluating progress: if we don't evaluate, how can we justify to ourselves, to ministers and to the public, that the strategy is working or indeed not working? The White Paper was fairly gentle on itself in terms of evaluation. I think that reflected the recognition that 3 years is a very short time for a strategy: no one is saying that by the end of 1997-98 the problem will have been fully grasped; it is a small period of time to deal with such a complex issue. But we have to start to establish some benchmarks nationally and locally, to give us some confidence as we move forward, so that we do know with a bit of clarity and evidence, before the end of that period, what should happen after it. That ties in with political issues. There will clearly be an election between now and 31st March 1998, and the extent to which the consensus could be preserved and developed will be a tested if results seem ambiguous or even depressing, in terms of what we are trying to achieve collectively. The Unit has an important role in trying to consult and work with others, so that what comes after 1998 makes sense. I would be hard pressed to be convinced that DATs and the whole DRG network and all those structures we have built up could suddenly just be cut off or disbanded at that point.

My final point underlying all of this, is an obvious one. We are looking at a problem that is dynamic. It is affected by many issues, in terms of how society develops, and particularly in the context of young people and how their lifestyles develop. Yet somehow, to achieve real progress over time, that dynamism has got to be related to a framework that is solid and consistent. This is a problem that is not going to vanish overnight, and it is going to require constant chipping away at. I hope that we can sustain a framework that facilitates that process.

THE SERVICE PROVIDER'S PERSPECTIVE

Roger Howard, Chief Executive, Standing Conference on Drug Abuse

When I was asked about nine months ago to speak today, *Tackling Drugs Together* was still in its infancy. Local Drug Action Teams were only just beginning to formulate their Action Plans and, indeed some had only just met. So it was with a degree of optimism that I agreed. Can I take this opportunity to applaud ISTD for its foresight and the quality of programme, speakers and presenters it has assembled.

Tackling Drugs Together also holds a special personal interest for me, not so much in my current capacity at SCODA but rather in a previous guise. Four years ago, I was commissioned by the Department of Health to report on practical steps which could be taken to improve collaboration to tackle drug misuse. Previous inter-agency arrangements, through local District Drug Advisory Committees were not working very well. I concluded and recommended that two major things were needed. One was effective co-ordination, at the national level, between government departments who, all too often, were seen as vying and jockeying for control over the drugs agenda. These disputes, and the virtual withdrawal from the process by the old Department for Education, meant a fragmented policy framework and the absence of a clear steer to local public services and others. Lack of leadership created a vacuum of opportunity. Now, wearing the service provider's hat, it is a matter of satisfaction that we have the CDCU in England and a new central unit in Wales.

The other principal recommendation was to sweep away the old local collaborative arrangements of District Drug Advisory Committees and replace them with new partnership arrangements, bringing together commissioners, purchasers, drug specialists and broader community interests. It was, and still is my view, that the issue of drugs, drug use and drug misuse is an issue for the entire fabric and infrastructure mechanism of local communities and not only professionals. Drug users are our - your - brothers, sisters, family, partners, close friends and next door neighbours. They are citizens with the same rights and responsibilities as other members of the community. We have enough forces at work adding more people to those who are socially excluded. Howard Parker (see page 19) has made clear the reality that the prevalence of drug use is now widespread. What we cannot ignore is the fact that technically, every one of these young people has committed a crime. To marginalise and potentially exclude from our society such an enormous number is morally indefensible and not workable. It is this reality that specialist drug services and of course others are now coping with. It is also encouraging that the Government has not only set up the DAT system but is now backing it up with, albeit modest, financial support.

Before I look at *Tacking Drugs Together: One Year On*, I think I ought first to clarify what I mean when I talk of drug service providers. The traditional definition focuses on those who provide the specialist drug treatment, rehabilitation and social care services - the drug dependency units, the residential rehabilitation services, the low threshold street agencies, the community drug teams, the syringe exchange schemes, the prison counselling support programmes, the structured day programmes and so on. Increasingly, we are seeing innovation and diversification. We have adult fostering schemes and detached floating support staff working in, and with, housing associations. But the service provider field has broadened to include those specialist organisations working in the fields of education and prevention. They are pioneering education and approaches to help young people learn about drugs in order that they can appraise the personal and wider risks of drug use. Those working on preventive approaches are engaging with local communities and, as Jud Barker explains (see page 69), pulling local criminal justice and treatment agencies together to ensure better co-ordinated and more effective responses.

I should also declare another interest in the Government's strategy and it is that the Standing Conference on Drug Abuse is looked to as an umbrella organisation to give voice to this diversity of services. It also looks to us to provide leadership in the areas of standards, accreditation of services, good practice development and promotion, and training development. So not only do I want *Tackling Drugs Together* to succeed but I also recognise we have a responsibility to help make it happen. I think it an illustration of the consultative process leading up to the White Paper and the recognition of the importance of the non-governmental sector that this strategy - perhaps for the first time in a governmental White Paper - recognises the real importance of partnerships with NGO's.

I also think it important to place *Tackling Drugs Together* in some historical context. It is not the

Government's first drugs strategy. We had the first in the late 1980s. It also had the opportunity to build on the very solid recommendations of the Advisory Council on the Misuse of Drugs which advises the Home Secretary.

The ACMD has, during the 1980s and 1990s, produced a series of influential reports looking at Treatment and Rehabilitation, Prevention, Education, Training, AIDS and Drug Misuse, Probation, Police and recently Prisons. Next year it will report on drug misuse and the social environment. We have also had important advice from the Health Advisory Service on substance misuse services for children and young people and, last month, a major review of the effectiveness of drug treatment services commissioned by the Department of Health. And of course, we have had a stream of reports from the Drug Advisory Service looking at service delivery and collaboration in local areas. Basically we have, as a backdrop, developing professional, political and public interests in the issue. Set this against the growth in drug use and effectively, *Tackling Drugs Together* is a logical and overdue outcome.

Positive achievements

So what are some of the good things about the strategy from a provider's perspective? I have identified what I believe are six key factors:

1. **National leadership and co-ordination**. In very simple terms, in the Lord President of the Council, those interested in drug misuse have a product champion, someone of senior cabinet rank, without the shackles of departmental responsibility or bias. Service providers do not work in isolation. They too span the boundaries of police, courts, probation, prisons, social services, education, health care, health promotion, housing, training and development and employment. Drug users' and misusers' needs do not fit neatly within institutional or organisational boundaries. Of course, all public services have to work across professional and institutional barriers. But, as the Health Advisory Service has commented in its report on children and young people, service development has been very fragmented and in some areas non-existent. The strength of the national leadership from a provider's perspective is that it lays the foundations and creates a national mechanism which we can seek to influence, not from the perspective of organisations, but rather from the needs of the individual and community. This national leadership and co-ordination also comes with some degree of accountability. In the last year or so alone, there have been three major parliamentary debates about drugs. Having said that I have to say I was appalled that only three members from the Labour opposition turned up for the latest five hour debate and drug misuse last Friday.

2. The second good thing is that local areas have, by and large, established **functioning DATs**. In some areas, the maturity and sense of genuine partnership has been apparent. Specialist drug service providers, especially from the voluntary sector have been brought onto the DATs. From what I hear, they have responded well to the challenge and responsibility. Of course I look on this as a good case of modelling behaviour. If we espouse partnership then it seems quite logical to me, that DATs should practice what they preach. The successful DATs, I believe, are drawing on the expertise and commitment of drug service providers in an inclusive rather than exclusive way. Providers and DATs can only benefit from this.

3. The third positive factor is that the output from DATs and individual organisational strategies is leading to a better recognition of the unique **strengths and contributions of specialist drug service providers**. Let me give you a couple of examples of this. The national prisons strategy accompanied by local prisons drug strategies has focused attention on this issue more than ever before. True, special initiatives sometimes skew local priorities and there is an overriding pre-occupation with the mandatory drug testing programme. Nevertheless, because specialist drug treatment providers have a long tradition of going into prisons, the prison service has looked to them to pioneer the setting up of the 20 plus, pilot prison treatment programmes. Of course there will be glitches, but the openness of so many prison staff and the willingness of providers to take risks in service development is leading to better partnerships and a service to those who need it.

   In the education field, we see some of the specialist drug education service providers providing advice and training to DAT members about their local education initiatives. Again, the mature or wise DAT recognises that it cannot achieve its goals without the support and help of specialist providers.

4. The fourth positive key factor is the **development of the demand reduction paradigm**. Put very simply, the 20th century history of responses to drug use and misuse has revealed a polarisation

between the treatment or medical interventions model and a criminalisation or punitive sanctions based response.

The developing paradigm of demand reduction compliments or perhaps contrasts, depending on how you wish to interpret it, with the supply side model of tackling drug use. This paradigm looks to education and prevention as a third leg of the stool. For those in the drug education and prevention area this can only be classed as good news. Of course others are not so convinced but one can understand their response in a very competitive environment for resources. There is much to develop in the demand reduction model which will stretch specialist drug service providers. But from our point of view, this emphasis in the strategy, accompanied by the de-facto support for harm minimisation efforts, really does offer recognition of the pioneering work specialist drug services have achieved over the past 20 years. I sense a growing recognition, one year on, of the unique contribution specialist providers can make.

5. A fifth encouraging key factor that service providers should not be churlish about, is the fact that there have been some modest **additional resources** made available. I know they may well have been taken away from other worthwhile social programmes. But I, we, have to accept the reality of this. It may be a card trick or a sleight of hand but, it has in our field, led to important developments. There are the ring fenced allocations to the prisons treatment programmes, the £6m for educational interventions, the £6m for new treatment for young people and methadone programmes, the new £2m challenge funds for DATs. They are not sufficient to cope with the rising need but, they are an advance on what we had before.

6. My final sixth positive factor on the good that has emerged from *Tackling Drugs Together* for providers is, ironically, about **public perception**. This may seem paradoxical when one reads the daily diatribe from some of the press about drugs and drug use. But the HEA information campaign, and public debate about strategy and policies, have generated increased media interest. I am sure all my colleagues here today will testify to that. Sometimes I have to confess it is a complete pain being patient with a tabloid journalist whose only apparent aim is to rubbish something. But I sometimes wonder whether, as the old saying goes, "all publicity is good publicity". In the London Borough of Lewisham recently they convened a citizens' jury to look at what should be done about drug misuse. In a survey of borough residents' concerns, drugs came out very high on the list of problems. At the outset, the jury was very much against decriminalisation or being soft on drug users and dealers. After about five days' work of hearing expert evidence from all sorts of people with very widely differing views, they reached the conclusion that decriminalisation should be explored and that much more treatment ought to be available for dependent drug users. Against an avalanche of publicity, they reached a conclusion quite contrary to perhaps what we might have expected. I mention this not to say they reached a right or wrong decision. Rather, from a service provider's point of view, I believe that *Tackling Drugs Together*, and the new public information campaign, have stimulated a debate which can be turned to our advantage. It can help lay the foundation for initiatives which steer people from the more punitive elements of the criminal justice system towards more constructive efforts to address the prevention and treatment of drug misuse. It also underpins the valuable work of family support groups, educational programmes working with schools and innovative drug prevention work.

So these are some of the ways in which the government strategy has achieved, and is achieving positive results for providers. But, there are also some shortcomings about the strategy which are not being addressed and there are forces at work which will make it doubly difficult for drug service providers and others to achieve their aims. Let me take each of these in turn.

The shortcomings of the strategy

Despite the now proven evidence of the effect of drug treatment in reducing criminal behaviour, there are no clear plans or targets to build a more even balance of the distribution of government expenditure. In 1993/94, the last year we have published figures for, two thirds of the Government's £520m spending on drug misuse went on enforcement and control measures. Only one third went on treatment and prevention.

In California, one of the largest research programmes into the effectiveness of drug and alcohol treatment carried out by the state government found that every dollar invested in treatment saved the taxpayer $7 mainly through reduced crime.

If the Government is serious about reducing the demand for drugs it will need, as Canada has done, to work towards a new balance of spending. A Home Office Minister recently announced that £77m of assets were confiscated last year. Home Office research has drawn attention to the ways by which this could be increased and the proceeds redistributed to local services. Across the UK this might amount to about £$^{1}/_{2}$m per Drug Action Team. Not an insignificant sum. This would be a start in shifting the balance towards prevention and treatment.

Tackling Drugs Together also does little to address the underlying association between deprivation, dependent drug use and associated crime. The 1994 British Crime Survey results, whilst showing that drug use per se is distributed throughout the social economic spectrum, also demonstrates the positive and powerful association between drug dependency, poor housing, unemployment and low income. 80-90% of drug misusers attending drug treatment services are long term unemployed. This is not surprising when they have been on heroin for 8 to 10 years. In a survey carried out in the north west of England in 1992, nearly 40% of those using drugs in public places were homeless. Nor does the strategy adequately reflect the cumulative and complex relationships of multiple need. Of a group of dependent opiate users admitted to one London drug clinic, 36% had been victims of sexual abuse. My service provider members repeatedly highlight the numbers coming to their attention who have been through the care system - 80% in some cases. And as the growing number of official enquiries into deaths such as the Jonathan Newby case in Oxford have illustrated, so many dependent drug users have mental health problems, alcohol problems, housing problems and so on. They end up in and out of services and, inevitably, prisons. Yet government is doing very little to address these problems through the drugs strategy.

And, despite the very worthy intentions of the community care arrangements which preceded *Tackling Drugs Together*, the strategy has not yet led to adequate improvements in that area. In fact, I worry whether we might be seeing a worsening of the situation.

SCODA recently carried out a survey of service providers across England and Wales looking at the implementation of community care, nearly 3 years on. Some of the findings are disappointing. We found:

- large differences between local authorities in assessment and care management arrangements
- 1 in 5 local authorities were reported in December last year to have used up their budgets for drug and alcohol misusers only three quarters of the way into the year
- whilst 70% of people referred for assessment were able to access residential placements, 30% were not. Is a 30% fall out rate reasonable?
- some local authorities were drawing eligibility criteria so tight as to exclude the carrying out of assessments before a person left prison - something explicitly contrary to ACMD and government guidance
- the fast track assessment procedure was so fast in some places that even after 3 months a decision had not been taken
- and drug misusers with dependent children were getting virtually nothing at all.

The other major fault line in the strategy is, of course, that it largely overlooks the foreign and major supply dimensions. I won't go into this, but an explicit domestic strategy needs to be matched with an international perspective.

Larger forces at work

I also mentioned that there were other forces at work which service providers view with grave misgiving because they are making or will make, our work so much more difficult. Let me briefly outline them.

One is the importation of the American response to crime. I suspect I do not need to say to this audience how cautious we must be in giving succour to our politicians' predilections in this area. Luckily, in the drug misuse field we do not suffer from this too much. Certainly there may be useful principles we can extract and apply in our particular European context, such as from the drug courts experience. But America has little to offer us in the way of tackling crime.

I suppose the obvious move in this advancing Americanisation, is the recent sentencing White Paper. Drug users and the minnow user-dealers get a double whammy here from the mandatory seven year proposals for a third drug trafficking or burglary conviction. We know dependent drug users thieve, so if they don't get caught up under the trafficking provisions they get sucked in through persistent burglary. Lord Chief Justice Taylor and Sir Peter Lloyd, a previous Conservative Home Office Minister, have both said these proposals will only lead to the imprisonment of minor drug dealers who are supplying to sustain their own drug use.

Another negative force is what's happening within the prison system. The inexorable rise in numbers coupled with the savage spending cuts will only make service providers' efforts more difficult. Through-care staffing is being cut and I really do not see in the long term how the current privileged central ring fenced status of the new pilot drug treatment programmes will be sustained. If devolved, will they go the same way as many of the prison education programmes? Destroy the constructive regime and you will inevitably get more drug use.

And talking of education, there are negative forces at work there as well. Despite the very welcome DfEE guidance to schools about drugs, this is being implemented against rising numbers of exclusions. I imagine the overwhelming majority of these are not drug related. But research by Portsmouth University has shown the risk of these excludees then being drawn into other more risky behaviours, including drug use.

Within the housing field we see also very worrying trends at work. Only recently, a craftily drafted amendment to Housing Benefit regulations was put forward by the Secretary of State for Social Security. Its impact would be devastating on those special needs housing bodies who have tried so hard over the past few years to develop provision for drug misusers, offenders and those with mental health problems. Many of our drug service providers working in this field have said they will have to close. And all because the right and left arms of government are working in diametrically opposed ways.

We even have the Labour Party putting forward amendments to the Housing Bill in order to evict dealers from housing estates. Don't they realise that again it will be the minnows, the user dealers, that will bear the brunt of this? And where do they expect them to go? It may sound tough on crime but it certainly does not tackle the causes of crime.

Next steps

Let me end by looking forward at some of the things service providers look for - perhaps in *Tackling Drugs Together Mark 2*. There are 5 things we could achieve.

1. We need to manage to break down the institutional barriers to the joint commissioning of services. It seems to me there is an uneasy truce between agencies about local spending patterns and responsibilities. We have, in effect, largely comfortable, compatible (not joint) commissioning. But, could we not achieve larger social gains through a significant re-alignment of spending patterns? How robust are the systems to achieve this? DATs are a unique model of inter-agency collaboration. We could use them to introduce a major innovative approach to the joint commissioning process.
2. Coupled with this, and as an example, I would hope service providers could see a major drive, in partnership with police, probation and the courts, to develop diversion into treatment services, whether these be cautioning plus, pre, or post sentence initiatives. I don't believe the police, magistrates or judges want to sentence people with drug problems without the opportunity for them to get help from services in the community. Let us use that community of interest and look to new ways of jointly commissioning these services. The criminal justice system is not the best place for people to get the help they need.
3. I also hope we will have a re-think about the purposes of drug education. At the moment we are setting it up to fail by looking to it to ensure that young people resist drugs. Against a tide of youth culture messages, that is hopelessly over-optimistic. Drug education and information is good in its own right. We teach history because it is a good thing to do and leads, hopefully, to better educated citizens. We don't do it in the hope it will, for example, prevent wars.
4. In the prevention arena we have to look at going upstream in young people's lives - something which perhaps takes us outside of the special contribution of drug services. A growing body of research has now highlighted the importance of early interventions work with families at high risk of having youngsters with psycho-social and delinquency problems. Significant numbers of these will end up as dependent drug users. We need to see new co-ordinated efforts on the early intervention and prevention front.
5. And finally, of course, service providers would like to see a more rational and sensible debate about the effectiveness of our drug laws. This is not about backdoor decriminalisation or legalisation.

Rather, it is a recognition that along with under age sex and under age drinking, drug use represents mass law breaking on a grand scale. If our laws are to mean anything, it is that we hope the overwhelming majority of the populace abide by them. But is the current construct of the law acting as an effective deterrent and as a means of punishment? It is over 25 years since the Misuse of Drugs Act was put on the statute book. At some point in the future, within our broad international obligations, we will need to find a new way of reconciling the reality of large scale drug use and our quest for social order, particularly set against the context of enormous community and family structural changes.

I started by highlighting the positive gains to have come out of *Tackling Drugs Together*. The shortcomings I have illustrated have to be taken account of. With central government co-ordinated leadership and local DATs, we do have a great opportunity to move forward. Service providers, who after all have struggled to get this issue on to the political and public service agenda for so long, have been rewarded. Can I end by urging all those on DATs or Drug Reference Groups to use their expertise to the full? They have so much to offer.

DRUG ACTION TEAMS' INFORMATION NEEDS
Anna Bradley, Director,
Institute for the Study of Drug Dependence

Summary
While much of the information required to support *Tackling Drugs Together* is obtainable, the systems for identifying local information and making it available are not yet well established. There may be a value for Drug Action Teams (DATs) in seeing their role as not just using or "purchasing" information, but also in providing it. DATs might wish to become the coordinators of information at a local level, identifying it and ensuring it is made available to all those who need it.

Introduction
In November 95, when everyone was hastily trying to come to terms with the *Tackling Drugs Together* (TDT) requirements to write action plans, I was asked to speak at three DAT chairs' conferences on the subject of DATs and information. In some ways we were as new to the game as the DATs and there was a strong element of common sense and second guessing in our suggestions.

However, ISDD has strong credentials in this field since our business is information. Our objective is to advance knowledge, understanding and policy making about drugs through information. More directly, since November ISDD has been working on a number of projects exploring DATs and information in great detail - two consultancies (Camden & Islington[1] and Sheffield), a three month focused CDCU/ HEA[2] project and currently some privately funded work thanks to Smith's Charity. As a result, I am able now to speak with more authority than last November, though happily what I have to say today is not substantively at variance with what I said then.

Some information basics
Most people who deal with information now understand that the value of information is in its use, rather than in its mere existence. This means that there is broad agreement about the need for all information to have four characteristics: it should be relevant, appropriate, accessible and credible.

Relevance - information needs to address the question that is being asked. In the case of DATs this implies, of course, that an appropriate question must be framed before information can be sought. Information must be collected with a purpose.

Appropriateness - information must be at a level and in a form that is appropriate for the questioner. This is particularly important for the DATs because the questioners are strategic generalists who have no time or inclination to become expert and need therefore to have information that is interpreted and summarised. Information for DATs also needs to be broad or multidisciplinary - across all thre TDT objectives *(community safety, young people and public health)* and it needs to give both a national and a local picture.

Accessibility - information should be easy to find. The sort of information required by DATs is often trapped inside local organisations and, while it is not confidential, it is not being made accessible either.

Credibility - Information needs to be believed. This isn't the same as requiring all information to meet the very highest of research standards, but rather ensuring that the quality of information is made transparent. In particular, anecdotal information from professionals in the field may be the very best intelligence available to a DAT, but it should always be presented as the observation it is, rather than as research.

ISDD's work with DATs has given us a much better picture of DAT information requirements and three aspects are particularly worthy of further exploration: the importance of collecting information with a purpose, the value of interpreted and summarised information and the availability of local and national information. It is these that I want now to explore in more detail.

Collecting with a purpose
DATs need to collect information with a specific purpose in mind rather than amassing information for its own sake. In their role as strategic planners, DATs will require information for:
- **P**roblem identification/prioritisation
- **A**udit of present activities/services/policies;
- **M**onitoring of processes, outputs and possibly outcomes.

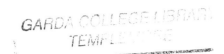

In reality the divisions made are artificial, ie PAM processes must occur in parallel, but the distinction is useful for the purposes of looking at DAT information needs,

Problem identification/prioritisation
Prioritising: - data to inform the planning process by demonstrating local need; information necessary for funding purposes; information for baselines. DATs may need:

Research studies. Local studies that would be useful include prevalence and local opinion surveys; needs assessments; drug service evaluations; and ethnographic studies of local drug scenes. National studies with regional breakdowns are helpful, eg Exeter Schools Survey, also studies conducted in other comparable localities.

Treatment statistics, crime statistics. National sources with regional breakdowns include: annual numbers of notifications of injecting users to the Home Office Addicts Index; numbers of new users presenting to services registered on the Regional Drug Misuse Databases. Local sources of statistics might include: A&E drug-related casualties, HIV and hepatitis figures, data from pharmacies and drug agencies, drug-related housing evictions, school exclusions, Coroner's Court mortality figures.

Anecdotal, soft data and intelligence. There are occasions when DATs will necessarily rely heavily on observations of professionals working with drug use or trafficking. These can be vital, used alongside and supporting hard data, in identifying new trends, catching problems early on and in setting up hypotheses for research.

Activities/implementing:- data to facilitate introductions between agencies; to indicate gaps in provision; to allow the sharing of good practice; to provide baselines for monitoring. DATs need:

Policy level: summary of DAT member agency roles and responsibilities. Information can include each agency's organisational structure, main roles and responsibilities, service targets, agency statement of intent regarding TDT and its own operational plans.

Mapping of local drug-related activities. Who is doing what? With whom? Where? And how much of each activity is there? This will include both drug specialist services', eg needle exchanges, and activities by non specialist agencies with drug related responsibilities, eg Probation Service supervision of drug using offenders. In addition to individual agency data, nationally/regionally available data on notifications of dependent users to the Home Office Addicts Index, or numbers of new users presenting to services and entered into a Regional Drug Misuse Database, may be viewed in part as indicators of activities by the agencies concerned.

Detailed implementation information relating to specific objectives in the DAT action plan. If, for example, the DAT has as an objective of 'ensuring all secondary schools have a drug coordinator', then whoever is taking the lead responsibility for implementation will need basic data on numbers of schools which currently have a coordinator, the name of contact person within each school etc.

Examples of good practice and effective interventions tried elsewhere. How has this issue been tackled in other areas? There is no need to reinvent the wheel. For example, good successful multi-agency partnership work around prevention, service provision, community safety.

Monitoring: - data to ensure quality assurance, efficiency and cost effectiveness and for future planning. DATs need to ensure that each action or objective in DAT action plans has at least one associated

performance indicator. For each objective there is a need for:
- *a nominated lead agency* with responsibility for ensuring the objective is taken forward,
- *a clear and agreed timescale* for measuring and reporting back to the DAT on progress,
- *agreement on anticipated outcome or output*, stated in terms of a specific, realistic (and possibly quite modest) measure of achievement,
- *baselines* - information indicating the state of play before an intervention takes place, and against which any output or outcome can be measured.

Interpreting and summarising
Information in its raw form is rarely of practical use to DATS. It needs to be interpreted, summarised and presented in a form that is digestible and usable for those taking decisions. The big question is, though, who will do the interpreting and summarising? Three possible interpreters suggest themselves and they all have their advantages and problems:
- the DAT Coordinator - the key issue here is time spent by the Coordinator and the opportunity cost in relation to other work s/he might be doing,,
- the information provider eg DMD -information providers are well placed to summarise their own information, but they may not understand the requirements of the DAT which will anyway end up with a handful of apparently unrelated summaries of information from the DMD, the police, the Prison Service, probation, etc,
- an external researcher/consultant - who may be able to give the overview better, but will be starting from a low knowledge base in relation to the DAT.

There is no obvious answer, but a solution needs to be found to suit each DAT and DRG.

Local and national
DATs will need to use both local and national sources to obtain the information they require. But given the nature of the DAT task it is not surprising to find that the balance of information is local, rather than national. In broad terms the split is as follows:
    local - research studies, treatment statistics, crime statistics, anecdote and intelligence, DAT member agency roles and responsibilities, mapping of service, implementation information, best practice, performance indicators and baselines,
    national - research studies, statistics with regional breakdowns, best practice, performance indicators.

Local information
Unfortunately for us all, however, while the national information requirements are reasonably well met, the local information is widely spread and not well managed. The grid below (see table I overleaf) shows how many, separate sources of information there are at local level. Much of this information is collected for internal/organisational reasons and is trapped there. It may not be in an appropriate form for wider dissemination (requiring some more work) and the organisation may not recognise the potential value of this information to others. If DATs are to be able to take advantage of this sort of information, they need a way to identify and then make it available - in short they need an information strategy.

An information strategy suggests something grand and complex. In fact it is simple, even common-sensical. It means asking the following questions about information:
- Why it is being collected?
- What needs to be collected?
- Where it will be collected - at local agencies or DATs?
- Who is going to take responsibility for collecting, aggregating, interpreting and summarising?
- When / how often will it be collected and reported on?

One possible solution is for the DAT to take on responsibility for developing an information strategy for its area, and in doing so take on some level of responsibility for coordinating the collection and interpretation of local information. But there are many ways to achieve a greater level of availability for local information, including some or all of the following possibilities:
- an audit of available local information within DAT priority areas. (This might be done through DRG members),

Table 1

Information Map - Local

	Community safety	Health & welfare	Education & prevention
Problems	Criminal justice agencies, LA surveys, Universities & Libraries.....	RDMD, drug agencies, health promotion.....	LEAs, schools, youth service, Drug Prevention Team, outreach projects, health promotion....
Activities	Criminal justice agencies, Crime Concern, LA - Community safety, housing, environmental health...	RDMD, Health/Drug Advisory Service reports, drug agencies, health promotion, community care plans...	DPI, health promotion, youth and education agencies...
Monitoring	Universities...	RDMD statistics, client outcome studies, Health of the Nation...	Specific evaluations

ISDD 26.6.96

Table 2

Information Map - National

	Community safety	Health & welfare	Education & prevention
Problems	Surveys collated by ISDD, Home Office (HO), Crime Statistics	Surveys collated by ISDD, HO, Addicts Index, RDMD	Episodic info from DfEE and OFSTED
Activities	HO & ACPO on activities, NACRO, ISDD and SCODA on best practice	Effectiveness Review, Health Advisory Service, SSI, SCODA, HPIC, NISW & ISDD	HPIC, NYA, NCB, TACADE, ISDD
Monitoring	TDT PIs	TDT PIs, specialist centres	TDT PIs

ISDD 26.6.96

- the development of a database or other information system for recording local information and its source,
- an information seminar for all those working within the DAT action plan,
- nominated information officers within each active agency ,
- an information reference group,
- a clear responsibility for information within the DAT co-ordinator's job description.

National information

There is much better coverage of information needs at a national level, but there are some gaps and many national information providers are not yet working to the DAT agenda. (See table 2).

The grid shows that there are far fewer sources of information at a national level and each of these provides information across a broader range. The problem is that many DATs do not yet know about these information sources. This is something that is being addressed in a report being circulated to DATs at this moment.

National information providers fall into two categories: those who are specialist in information relating to drugs (ISDD and SCODA),and those who specialise in some other subject area(s), which are relevant to drugs, but which do not require an understanding of drug issues, e.g. NACRO and the National Institute of Social Work (NISW). DATs need information of both types, but some of the national information providers do not see the value for DATs of the information they have.

In quality terms the national information network in the community safety area needs improving and there is a need for someone to take responsibility for providing ongoing information describing what is going on in education and prevention. But most importantly for DATS, there is a need for better access to local information from other areas. This would allow DATs to compare their situation with others and find parallels and new ideas.

Some solutions?

ISDD have been funded by Smith's Trust to address some of the weaknesses in the information available to DATS. We hope to work with a selection of DATs to establish whether the following services would be useful, and if so what shape they should take:
- World Wide Web pages on the Internet - ISDD already has a home page, but the idea here is to develop some pages which specifically address DAT information needs, perhaps with the potential for discussion groups and informal exchanges between DATs,
- A directory or handbook for DATs - a looseleaf publication containing key information for DATs and DRGs. (This might include basic drug facts, contacts for national information, contacts for DAT coordinators, funding sources, etc),
- Improved collection of local research - we want to work with some DATs to identify local research and ensure that ISDD can make this information available to people outside a locality for comparative purposes, and to spread good ideas.

Conclusion

- DATs require information that is focused and designed for strategic decision making.
- Much of the information that they require is local.
- Local information is scattered and often unknown or inaccessible.
- National information exists but is not always made known to DATS. There are some gaps.
- There could be a role for DATs in coordinating information at a local level.

Notes

1   Dorn, N & Mounteney, J. (March 1996) "Tackling Drugs Strategically" a consultancy report to Camden and Islington Health Authority from ISDD. Available from Camden and Islington DAT.

2   Mounteney, J and Dorn, N. (May 1996) "Tackling Drugs Informatively". Report to the CDCU/HEA from ISDD on DAT information needs. Available at £5.00 for single copies, £2.50 for orders of five or more from ISDD, 32 Loman Street, London SE1 OEE.

ADOLESCENT DRUGS PATHWAYS IN THE 1990's

Professor Howard Parker, Manchester University

What I want to talk about today is the background of *Tackling Drugs Together*, which is young people and drug use. One thing I have to say about *Tackling Drugs Together* is that I object strongly to the handcuffing together of youth, drugs, crime and danger, as if every time a fifteen year old girl smokes cannabis she becomes a burglar or whatever. There is no relationship whatsoever, other than breaking the Misuse of Drugs Act, between youthful drug use and crime, and I think it is a great shame that *Tackling Drugs Together* has got this misleading theme. Basically what the Government did was confuse heroin use and crime in the 80s with recreational drug use and young people in the 90s.

Firstly what are the key drugs arenas at the moment? Of course there are several million alcohol, tobacco and cannabis users, but the scene I am talking about today is 'adolescent recreational drug use'. Then at the end, because the cohort study I will talk about are 18 years old this year, they are moving into the young adult, rave party, university, staying out all night, not telling your parents where you are, scene, I think we ought to look at the young adult drug scene as well. Obviously Ecstasy (MDMA) is prominent here, though I will suggest that cocaine is now slipping into this arena. There are also the 80s/90s heavy heroin lifestyles. That is where the drug/crime connection is strongest. And I think there is another issue about poly-drug use, led on by crack or rock cocaine. What we found in our study was that the crack cocaine users in the North West were poly-drug users, and whilst they used crack cocaine as their primary drug, they used heroin to manage the come-down effect.

We conducted a five year study of what were 700 but are now 550 young people from the age of 14 through the five years to this year, when they are 18[1]. We are still working on the fifth year results so I will only be talking about the 4th year findings today. What we are able to do through this longitudinal study, is to look at how people change, how they make decisions, how they review those decisions, hence the title '*Adolescent Drugs Pathways*'. Each year we followed these 14, 15, 16, 17, 18 year olds through questionnaires and last year we interviewed nearly 100 of them. We tried to interview a representative sample with different pathways; abstainers, drug users and so on.

We are also looking at 'critical incidents' this year with them. Where they have a major incident they try to let us know and we try to interview them. Some of these have been funny, some have been sad and some of them have been dangerous and worrying. We have one young woman in a South American prison from our cohort who foolishly went on a holiday and was persuaded by a male companion to 'donkey' (smuggle) some drugs and she has got a seven year sentence. We are reading the transcripts now and trying to make sense of them, and it has given me a very strong sense of the kind of decisions that young people are making.

Drug offers and drug use

The bar chart (Fig 1) is based on the first 4 years of the study and the fourth group of bars shows rates of drug offers; that is, have you been in situations where drugs are available for free from friends or to buy? By year 4 it is 90%, right across the board. Gender and class are not very significant.

I am advancing a thesis of normalisation. Basically, now, we cannot find groups of young people other than Asian Muslims and a minority of very strong minded abstainers who are anti-drug use. There are people who are in 'offer' situations, or their friends take drugs, who do not want to take drugs, and they do not feel under pressure at 16 or 17 to do so. They have their own position, and that is one of the aspects of normalisation. Another is the ready availability of drugs in the 1990s, which I am sure you are aware of. It is something new and we must remember that this generation is the first generation to grow up in a situation where drugs are freely available in all the social space they move in.

The first three groups of bars show drug taking figures for the four years, based on a sample of about 500 for years three and four and you can see that there is an increase in levels of use each successive year. Use of cannabis, poppers and LSD has gone up, but not solvents. It is interesting that the death rate for solvents and gas for England and Wales has gone down from 150 young people a year to around 50, and that is because most initial drug use is now with poppers or cannabis which are far less dangerous. It seems likely that the ready availability of cannabis is reducing deaths. For 11 and 12 year olds, the early users, this means they are much less likely to do themselves any harm in their first experimental

Figure 1

Drug use prevalence, offers and uptake for the cohort

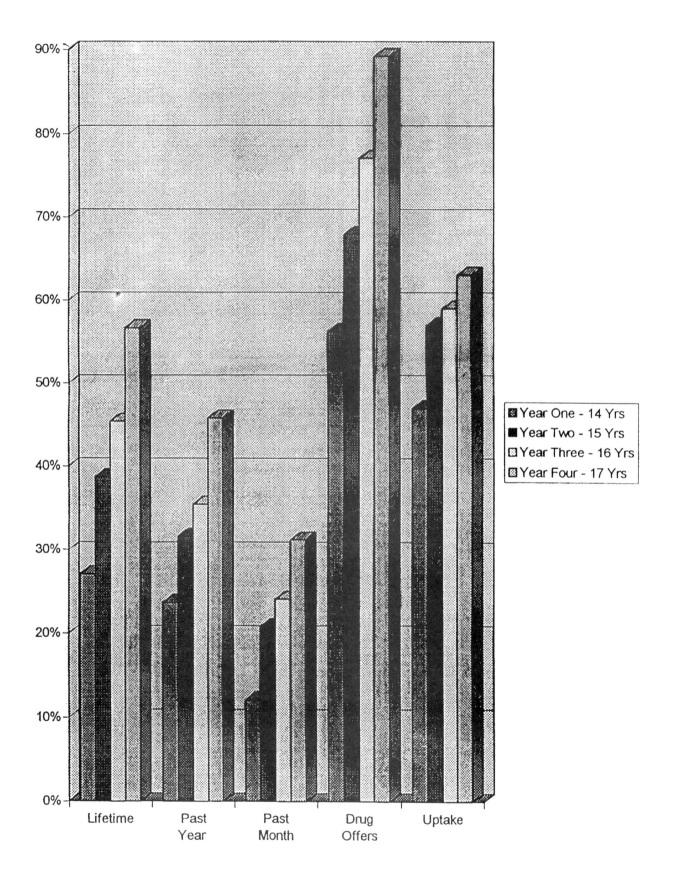

drug occasion than if they used butane gas or a fire extinguisher. There is a rise in amphetamine use, but it is the MDMA/Ecstasy figure that shows the sharpest rise. It will be over 20% in year 5. MDMA/Ecstasy is moving out of the dance club scenes into the normal social world of recreational drug use.

Our fifth year figures so far are based on just 450 returns. There will be about 530 when we have finished. We got more back this year. We are giving £10 CD tokens if you return the questionnaire this year. We get people who missed last year ringing us up saying, "Where the hell's the questionnaire? I want my CD token". When I started research I never thought that giving incentives would be an acceptable method, but I am afraid I have had to move with the times - it is amazing how little attrition you get when you give a CD token as a reward. Our results indicate that in year 4 a third of our representative sample by gender and social class have tried a drug in the last month. But they are still very much recreational drug users by and large.

This is not an exceptional sample. The survey results that we had in the first two or three years are now being replicated in all the other snapshot surveys. Obviously ours is a longitudinal study, but all the snapshot surveys - one has just been done in Wales, and others in Scotland - are picking up exactly the same figures as we are, so I would regard this as a typical example of a semi-urban population. Four of our original schools are highly successful state schools. The Sunday Times recommends you to send your son or daughter to one of them, for an excellent education. It does not mention that a third of the lower sixth smoke cannabis most weekends.

The bar chart shows the availability of drugs and whether people take the opportunity. Our uptake analysis shows clearly that if drugs are readily available you get more people taking them. It seems banal, but actually it is very important, because it is one of the major factors in explaining this generation's drug use. The drugs are there and they were not before, and there is nothing we can do about it, because there is now a very strong demand as well.

Drug pathways

I now want to talk about the pathways that young people in this sample are taking. There are four very clear groups (Fig 2). There are *current drug users*, most of whom have been using drugs for two or three years; a lovely little group called *ex-users*, who tried experimenting or using drugs at 14 or 15, and have now decided that drugs are not for them, and they do not want to use drugs again; a group that we call *'in transition'*, which is a large group: they may or may not have tried drugs but they do not regard themselves as drug users, they do not use drugs regularly; and there are some who have not used drugs, but what they have in common is that they think it likely they will use drugs in the future: so these are a group of seventeen year olds, some of whom have only used drugs once or twice, some who have never used drugs, saying in answer to the question 'Do you think you may use drugs in the future?' - 'Probably'. 'Which drug is it likely to be?' - 'Cannabis', followed by Ecstasy as a second drug. A lot of them expected to go to college last Autumn, about a third of the sample, and they saw leaving home, going to college, as a likely time for the onset of drug use.

What our analysis shows is a far more complicated and far more dynamic situation than for instance, *Tackling Drugs Together* implies. We have tended to think of 14 or 15 as the age of onset, but we are finding onset (that is first time drug use) just as likely at 17 or 18. You cannot explain that as adolescent rebellion or youthful curiosity - these are young adults making decisions about drugs. That confirms my normalisation thesis.

The fourth group is the *abstainers*, who have never tried an illicit drug and do not expect to in the future. These are rock solid now, this group. They have gone through adolescence not taking drugs. They are saying - "I do not ever expect to take a drug; I think people who take drugs are silly; you don't need drugs, you can have a good time without drugs, drugs are dangerous, drugs will kill you, drugs are illegal, drugs will spoil your life, your family, your career." They are very strong abstainers and my guess is that they will always be so. They are also very low-level smokers and drinkers. I think perhaps we are seeing a personality style or a way that people have been brought up. There are a lot of religious and moral rules that are put forward by this group, and they seem strongly influenced by abstentionist parents as well. They would be horrified to take drugs, for their parents to find out, because in their view that would destroy their relationship with their family. In other words, their families are solid abstainers as well. So, those are the four groups, and the four pathways down which people are going. But the pathways are changing and getting more complicated. If you add the current users and the ex-users and the 'in transition' together, there is only a third of the sample left that will say, 'I will never use drugs'.

Figure 2

Percentage of sample on different pathways

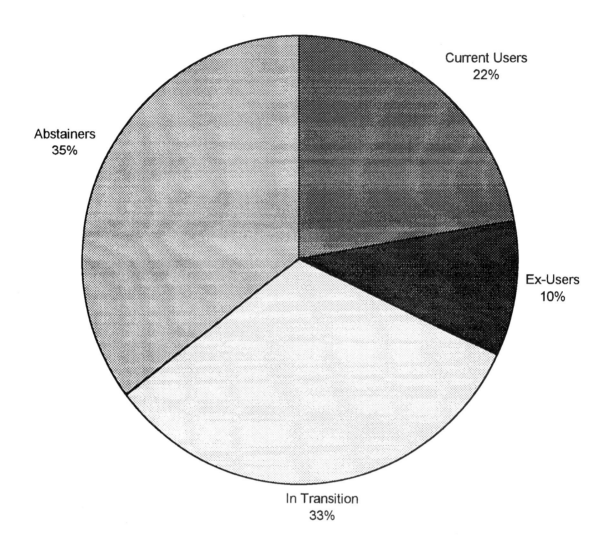

Apart from them there are a small number of users, or people who have tried drugs and quite a few who have said they might use drugs in the future. The ex-users are more like the abstainers because they have said "I have done drugs or I have tried drugs. Whatever that thing was I smoked, or that tablet I took - it was horrible and I'm not doing it again". So the ex-users and abstainers have more in common with each other than with the other two groups.

Let us look at these pathways. There is a small group that have tried drugs in the past and do not intend to try drugs again. We could see them as past experimenters. When you interview them they say "I was around at my mate's and my cousin rolled a spliff and passed it round, and we all tried it and I tried it, and then they had another one and I smoked that but I didn't like it" - or something like that. Or an ex-user may be someone who once took cannabis and then used an acid blotter, an LSD trip, and found that was OK a couple of times, but then the next time they had a horrible, paranoid, frightening experience and that finished them off. Because they do not smoke they do not see cannabis as a likely drug that they would use. The ex-users are more likely to have had negative or bad early drug experiences than current users and those in transition. Most have not taken drugs for the last two or three years. I think it is fair to call them ex-users even at 17.

The abstainers are a large group who do not intend to try drugs and are anti-drugs usually, although what we are finding is that as they get older they are much more likely to say - 'it's up to other people if they take drugs'. Quite a few of them have friends or acquaintances who are drug users or occasional drug users and by and large they are tolerant of this. Basically they do not see it as a major problem. They are least likely to be in drug offer situations. They are more home based, and they are more family focused as well.

Current users

The current users are becoming a bigger group all the time. Our analysis shows they have a mean number of drugs episodes of 8.5 in the past month. They are not using drugs every day. They are week-end users or for cannabis perhaps smoking it about two or three times a week. They identify with the statement 'I take drugs, I think drug taking is OK if you're careful and you know what you're doing', and they expect to continue taking drugs. They have got pro-drug attitudes - most of them think cannabis should be decriminalised. In the interviews we ask them 'If you could go on television for quarter of an hour and say something about drugs, what would you say?' and we get some absolutely fabulous cameos. Nearly all the drug users want to slag off the Government and people over 30 for being hypo-critical, and to decriminalise cannabis. Very few of them want to legalise other drugs. They are not mad, liberalising, decriminalising free marketeers; they are just saying from their experience at 17 or 18 they cannot see the point in cannabis being illegal, when other drugs like alcohol and tobacco are legal. They think we should go soft on soft drugs and go hard on hard drugs. That kind of message, is not quite in line with *Tackling Drugs Together*.

The key drugs are cannabis, amphetamines, the poppers, LSD and Ecstasy (MDMA). What we are starting to find, in all the drug scenes, is the beginning of *poly-drug use*. Use of alcohol/cannabis is almost basic now, at weekends. People drink and take cannabis, and when they go clubbing they drink and take amphetamines and Ecstasy. Then they might well use cannabis in the early hours of next morn-ing to get themselves to sleep. What seems to have happened in the night club scene in the north west, (I am thinking of one particular working class group) is that everyone still gets absolutely legless, occa-sionally fights and gets a taxi home with their mate or whatever, but they also now use tablets in the middle of all this. So the pure 'huggy-lovey' Ecstasy-only night clubs are not a feature. The clientele in our sample tend to go to the local town club which is just as it has always been, except that there is Ecstasy as well. I am sorry to spoil any cuddly images of MDMA but after 5 bottles of 'Bud' the MDMA tends not to have such a good effect on you anyway. A lot of people mention having to take mates home or taking mates to hospital. The non-drug users who go to the clubs cannot understand why people want to spend twenty-five or thirty quid on tablets, drink 'designer' cider or lager and then sit totally numbed in the corner until they are kicked out. They do not see that as particularly good value. We may find that MDMA, alcohol, cannabis, amphetamines and LSD on the same night do not mix. If there is a health message for the second phase of *Tackling Drugs Together* perhaps this should be it. Poly drug use will become a significant problem.

I find the 'in transition' group, fascinating. They are working out their perspectives on drugs. I suggest that the early drug users were also early drinkers and early tobacco users. n other words you can predict drug use at 13, 14 through early risk taking, and that works for 14, 15, 16. But at 17 and 18, there are nice girls from nice homes, with nice parents and nice families, getting nice 'A' level results, going to nice quiet campus universities, starting to take drugs, and they were not early smokers, they do not smoke, they were not early drinkers, though they drink now. They are not delinquent, they have no criminal records, they are highly successful, academic people, extremely well adjusted, extremely articu-late. They are self assertive. They are now starting to take drugs or they are saying 'I will this year, or next'. In Manchester where there are over thirty thousand students, at about 15 colleges and universities, all the clubs have 'Freshers Rave Week' in the second week in September. You register, you unpack your trunk, wave off Mummy in the Volvo, and then get your tickets for the induction programme which is the Hacienda or Paradise Factory and so on. You do not walk around the student union saying '... and there are the social clubs and there is the badminton court'. People want to get their tickets to go to the Hacienda, because that *is* Freshers Week. All sorts of rubbish is sold in these clubs in the first week until students get a bit wiser. Many of this 'in transition' group are exactly at this point. They went to Univer-sity in the Autumn and they expect their lives to get more exciting. They absolutely slogged it over 'A' levels. A number of them say 'I only smoked cannabis over 'A' levels because I don't want to ruin my sleep patterns, I want to sleep properly. I don't do anything else, I've not done any dancing, I've not done any amphetamine. If I think cannabis is slowing me down, I think, I'll go back to my lager or whatever'. Many of them thought it helped them not to get stressed out, a bit of drinking, a bit of cannabis, but they left all the weekend stuff alone while they were doing 'A' levels. This is not the sign of a disorganised person, a disordered, drug crazed, failing, delinquent, street corner person. This is not the classic adolescent pattern. We cannot say it is about curiosity and rebelliousness because the onset is now into young adulthood. That is another indication of normalisation.

Commodification and consumption

It is exactly the same in young people's drinking as it is in their drug use. There is more and more variety, there are more and more products. They are specifically designed for the market, cleverly packaged, sold in small containers and they have a hell of a kick. Another clear development at the moment in the adolescent drugs scene is that alcohol and drugs are seen to go together to produce 'getting wrecked', 'getting out of it', 'off my head', 'blasted'. 'Did you have a good time?' 'I think so but I was wrecked.' 'Do you know anything about standard units of alcohol?' 'Yes, if I can stand up I haven't had enough to drink; if I fall over I've had too much'.

It is about consumption. This generation see drugs as another thing to consume. They are not buying drugs to annoy the headmistress, they are buying drugs because they want to try them, because they want to take them, because they like the effects, because it helps them cope with the rhythms of their lives. Some become problem users but many see drug use fitting into the rhythms of their life and in the same way as earlier generations, ('I've had a bad day at the office') have gone straight to a bottle of wine or scotch.

I find the smoking figures really depressing. After all the health education, young women are smoking more and more. A third of the sample are smokers, and young women are smoking more than young men. Let us compare smoking with drugs pathways. Drug abstainers do not smoke, ex-users do not smoke very much. Two-thirds of current drug users smoke. It seems the tendency for people to use psycho-active drugs is a kind of clustered thing to do with their lifestyles. Early smoking and drinking can be linked with delinquency and sexual activity as well. But we found another set of motivational accounts and decision making comes into play after the age of 15, and I think that means that drug use is not going to remain related to adolescence. It will grow up with this generation and they will continue to be drug users or not, but certainly over half of them in my view will continue to use drugs well into their 20s. This comes with the delay in settling down, in having children, in having their own home, in being financially independent. We are creating *post adolescence* now from about 18 to 24/25. Most young people are in this 'other' status, not fully independent adults, a lot of them still living at home, but a lot of them have personal freedom and they are consumers. They will reject changing their drug repertoire and losing this 'time out', this little space, amid the stresses and strains of life, so drugs will be here to stay.

Ecstasy

I am worried about MDMA, much more than any of the other drugs. It has come from the pay party, dance, night clubbing scene. We know from research, that on the dance floor most people take more than one drug. They might take two or three in a typical night. We know that from the Scottish research in particular. But what is starting to happen now is that Ecstasy is extending beyond the dance club scene, down into the adolescent recreational drug scene and we noticed a sharp rise in incidents with MDMA from the age of 18. The dangers of the drug are unclear and will remain so for several years. We know in monkeys and rats that the serotonin flood that MDMA stimulates damages neural pathways. We know that the centres of the brain where that happens are the centres that relate to empathy and calmness, but also to depression. So as John Henry has said, we are involved in a massive social experiment with the generation of young people who are dropping these pills down their throats every week. We cannot know what will happen. What is very clear this year from our research is that a lot of people are having very bad incidents because of mixing tablets up with all the other things that they tend to consume over the weekend. We are getting a lot of reports of bad experiences, of having to take friends to hospital and I think that is because of poly-drug use. The fact is that MDMA is too powerful. You really should not mix it with all the other things that they want to mix it with on a Friday and Saturday night.

The normalisation of recreational drug use

Normalisation does not mean that it is normal for all young people to take drugs. It means that those who do not take drugs accept those who do, and accept that drugs are around and do not call the police or tell the teachers or anything. They just leave it alone. The thesis we started to test a couple of years ago was that normalisation was taking place in relation to recreational drug use. There is widespread availability and choice typical of the massive consumption pattern of this growing-up generation. Early onset would suggest normalisation, and it is there. What we have also found is late onset.

Tackling Drugs Together talks about targeting children younger, starting in primary school, or nursery school. And yet we are finding young people without any of these deviant tags on them starting drug use at 17 and 18. That is another sign of normalisation, when the successful, particularly academically successful, non-delinquent, non-early-risk-taking young people, see recreational drug use as part of their repertoire of life. We are finding that the abstainers, who used to write really rude things about drug users when they were 15 or 16, are now being much more mellow about it. They are now saying, 'Well, they don't give me any hassle, I don't give them any hassle. Obviously when I go out to a club or a party I see this stuff going on all the time. It's not for me and people don't give me any hassle". That is a more mature approach, and it indicates normalisation.

Drug use is to do with preference rather than peer pressure. I think the recreational drug scene will start to merge now with the young adult dance drugs scene and, what is more worrying, I expect cocaine to appear soon in the dance drug scene. Certainly in the North West and in London, there is evidence now of cocaine appearing on the dance floor, so I think what used to be separate drugs arenas are starting to mesh. In our Crack Cocaine Study[2] we found most of the crack cocaine users were poly-drug users. This also applied in a study coming out on methadone maintenance[3] where we had a control group in the community in Merseyside who wanted treatment. They were poly-drug users in their late twenties. So poly-drug use, and sequential drug use, using different drugs for different reasons, seems to be becoming a kind of accepted pattern of use for all groups. If I can put it in the old fashioned terms, you get drunk one night, you have two paracetamol and you go to work and drink four glasses of water. You are using water and paracetamol to modify the fact that you had too much to drink. If you are a drug user, you might take amphetamine or MDMA, you cannot sleep, so you take a depressant drug to help you sleep. It is the same with crack cocaine users, when they are totally wired and they cannot get down, they use heroin or methadone to pull themselves down again; so they are actually using other drugs as a kind of self-medication. I think that is what is going on now, at the top end of our recreational drug use scene and the dance scene. People think they can get away with it by spending £60 or £70 and just have a blissful 48 hours and every time one of the highs or one of the OKs starts to disappear you take another drug to compensate for it. It is logical, it comes very much with the notion of modern medicine I suppose. That does not make it good for you though.

Alcohol and problem drug use

My conclusion is that while a lot of recreational drug users will get drugs to fit into the rhythms of their life, a minority will turn out to be problem users. The problems will be greater because more drugs are available and because their expectations of what these drugs can do are much greater. So my guess is that we will have to start providing services, not for all young people who take drugs, but for young people who are misusing drugs in the sense that the drugs are starting to mess them up in various ways. Interestingly we asked a lot of questions in the survey about different drugs and what causes problems. The answers were: cannabis hardly any, amphetamines very few, LSD quite high and, my prediction is, this year, Ecstasy quite high. It is the lack of care, not respecting these psycho-active substances particularly after a few drinks, which is one of the major causes of the problems that Accident and Emergency departments see. There were so many interviews where people have said, 'I've no idea I was pissed.' 'What did you take? How many did you take?' 'I've no idea. I was pissed.' The drinks industry might not like this but if you are looking for a gateway drug to drug use it is alcohol. Whereas official policy says that it is cannabis, in reality it is alcohol. Now are we going to ban alcohol? I think not!

1. *Drugs Futures: changing patterns of drug use amongst English youth.* Parker H, Aldridge J and Measham F ISDD 1995
2. *Crack Cocaine and Drugs Crime Cameos* Parker, H and Bottomley T, Home Office Publications Unit, 1996
3. *Methadone Maintenance and Crime Reducation in Merseyside* Parker H, and Kirby P, Police Research Group, Home Office 1996.

RESPONDING TO THE REALITY OF DRUGS
IN YOUNG PEOPLE'S LIVES

Mark Gilman,Director of Research, Lifeline Project

This talk is about the place and meaning of drugs in young people's lives in 1996. So what qualifies me to talk about this subject? Well I would claim some expertise on the grounds of the 10 years that I have spent researching drugs in the north of England. But most important is the fact that I remain fascinated by British youth culture. In my opinion British youth culture is the most imaginative and vibrant youth culture anywhere in the world. With due respect to the African American youth living in the USA I think that British youth creates cultures that spread throughout the world. Moreover it is often British working class youth that are right at the centre of youth culture. British youth cultures are one of our most successful exports. These youth cultures have never, ever been so influenced by the use of illegal drugs.

In fact so widespread is the influence of illegal drugs that I would argue that contemporary youth culture is, in large part, a drug culture. British youth did not invent Ecstasy, but once they discovered it, they re-invented it as a dance drug. They created rave culture and they exported Ecstasy-inspired dance music all over the globe. It is this penetration of drugs into mainstream youth culture that is new. Drug use itself is not new. We had it in the 60s, the 70s and the 80s. But we have never, ever seen anything like the 1990s explosion in drug use. What is happening now is unprecedented, according to Howard Parker and his colleagues at the University of Manchester. If you reach your 16th birthday, living in the urban north west, and you have not used at least one illegal drug (usually cannabis), then you are a social deviant. Statistically speaking, the non drug user is now the abnormal one. Now that is new.

But if that is the bad news then the good news is that this massive increase in young people's drug use is largely explained by an explosion in the recreational use of the softer drugs such as cannabis, LSD, orally administered amphetamines and Ecstasy. The use of the classic drugs of addiction - heroin and, to a lesser extent, crack cocaine - is also on the increase. But the use of the harder drugs like heroin and crack means something completely different to young people who use drugs recreationally. For example, we have just conducted a survey of over 3,000 young recreational drug users who regularly use Ecstasy at dance clubs or raves. These young Ecstasy users hold some of the most extreme anti-heroin and anti-'junkie' attitudes that you will find anywhere. For the young Ecstasy users heroin addicts are sad people with whom they have nothing in common. In fact one of the clearest expressions of this key distinction between recreational drug use and drug addiction is seen when young Ecstasy users claim that they have more in common with people who do not use drugs than they ever have with addicts.

And yet we, as adults, insist on speaking to young recreational drug users as if they are all tomorrow's addicts. Young recreational drug users are no more likely to be tomorrows addicts than today's young alcohol drinkers are likely to be tomorrow's alcoholics. Consider this - how many of us had a glass of lager or cider or a bottle of Babycham at teenage parties? And how many of us have ended up drinking methylated spirits in bus stations? It is exactly the same with illegal drugs. Recreational drug use and drug addiction mean two completely different things. Recreational drug use and drug addiction occupy completely different places in the lives of young people. In order to be consistent and effective in providing drugs education we must distinguish between them.

We also need to look at those young people - that large minority of young people - who do not use drugs and have no intention of doing so. What influenced their decisions not to use? Is it because they have been taught to see drugs as bad? Have they accepted the message that comes from the life education centres, namely that drugs are bad because they damage people physically, emotionally, spiritually and socially. Or have they been taught that drugs are just plain wrong - that drugs are morally the wrong thing to do? Have they accepted the message that drugs are illegal because they are bad? They are not bad because they are illegal. This is certainly the line that was taken during the Reagan years in the USA when it was claimed drug use fell considerably. The much criticised 'Just Say No!' campaign was success-ful - say its supporters - precisely because it was an unambiguous moral crusade against the evils of drugs. Do we want a moral crusade against drugs?

So, we have looked at the recreational drug users and we have nodded in the direction of the non drug users. OK, but who then are tomorrow's addicts? Where will we find them? What do we need to look out for? Well in my opinion you can do worse than look at those white working class boys that the

Chief Inspector of Schools found to be right at the bottom of the educational pile. You will find tomorrow's addicts wherever you find poverty of opportunity. You will find tomorrow's addicts wherever you find chronic unemployment, you will find tomorrow's addicts wherever you find young people who have been abused by the modern world. These abuses may be physical, sexual or emotional in nature. They may have been caused by predatory adults. But wherever you find sad, unhappy people it is there that you will find tomorrow's addicts. Recreational drug use runs right across the boundaries of race, class and gender. But drug addiction runs along the fault-lines of our society. Contrary to popular belief one of the last places that you will find these sad and unhappy people is taking Ecstasy and dancing to house music at a rave.

These young recreational drug users are 'shiny happy people'. They are targeted by advertisers who use drug related language and drug imagery to sell their product. They have disposable income. They are not tomorrow's addicts, they are tomorrow's ordinary citizens exactly like we were when we were young. They are active consumers. Consequently, a certain pair of training shoes will provide the 'ultimate head trip'. A computer software firm will 'supply speed to techno junkies'. I have yet to see adverts that target drug addicts. This is precisely because drug addicts are going nowhere economically. All their disposable income is already spoken for.

In a study in Sheffield they found that today's recreational drug users who are still in school could easily imagine a time in the future when they would not be using drugs. The same study found that young people of the same age who were in the care of the social services were reluctant to even discuss the future. And this again highlights the difference between recreational drug use and addiction. I agree with the Health Advisory Service that in 1996 recreational drug use is 'normative behaviour'. It is just a part of growing up. Drug addiction on the other hand is not normal. Drug addiction only 'fits' - only makes sense - only means anything to people who are desperately unhappy. People who are going nowhere. Drug addiction - to paraphrase William Burroughs - 'Wins by Default'.

I would like to end by asking you to be very critical of the often assumed relationship between drugs education and drugs prevention. Many people believe that drugs education will prevent drug use. I have seen no evidence to support this. It is simply a case of wish fulfilment. I believe that drugs education is important, in and of itself, whether or not it prevents drug use.

PROVISION OF DRUG AND ALCOHOL SERVICES FOR YOUNG PEOPLE

Eilish Gilvarry, Clinical Director of the Northern Regional Alcohol and Drug Unit, Newcastle upon Tyne

The seminar discussed current trends of drug and alcohol use/misuse among young people. These include: the increased use of a wide range of drugs by the younger age group; increasing use among girls; the emergence of poly-drug use as the norm: and lowering of the age of initiation into substance use. Young people are growing up in a culture where drugs are more available and acceptable, and their consumption is perceived to be normal by their peer group. It is important to being clear about the nature of the problem and definitions commonly used. The Health Advisory Service noted that while use of drugs was undesirable because of users' increased exposure to potential social, psychological and physical problems, experimentation alone cannot be seen as indicative of personal disorder and should not be styled as misuse. The term 'misuse' was defined as use that is harmful, dependent use or the use of substances as part of a wider spectrum of problematic or harmful behaviour. Young people who misuse substances may also have significant problems with their psychosocial development.

There is a lack of leadership in both the commissioning and the provision of young people's services. Responses are poorly planned and poorly co-ordinated with pockets of isolated existence throughout the country. Professionals fail to recognise the particular needs arising from substance use and misuse by young people. There is limited specialised treatment, lack of definition and understanding of the problem, unclear and disputed funding responsibilities and competitiveness and lack of trust between existing service sectors and service components. Services and interventions where they exist have been developed in an isolated, patchy and idiosyncratic manner, usually by interested personalities. Young people's services need to be accessible, appropriate, youth orientated services, not just a modified version of a service provided for adult substance misusers. A four tiered strategic framework of service provision was put forward and discussed, similar to that presented in the HAS report.

The components of good practice in delivery of service for children and adolescents who misuse substances were discussed. The key principles could be: accessibility, appropriateness, lawfulness, competence of staff, respect for and protection of children and adolescents, collaboration, co-ordination, effectiveness, targeting and rigorous evaluation. The issue of confidentiality, consent to treatment and, in particular, the availability of syringe needle exchanges to under 16 year olds were discussed. Clear guidelines should be provided within a structure, particularly for outreach workers and others working with under 16 year olds. Examples of models of practice were discussed. These ranged from a one-stop-shop to various models of collaboration between child mental health services and adult addiction services.

Vulnerable young people with multiple problems should be targeted. They include children or young people who are in care, young offenders, the homeless, prostitutes, children whose parents have significant drug or alcohol problems, truants from school and those with problematic and/or dependent drug use.

Social services departments with their wide range of powers to care for and protect children and young people should also be developing services within their Children's Services Plans. There is a need for collaboration between local authority, health, housing and education and an end to fragmentation of services. Within this spirit of collaboration there is a need for:

- An accurate knowledge base about the problems and issues
- an overarching commissioning strategy that generates an approach to purchasing in which service specifications seek specific standards of service from a mix of provider services
- recognition of the multi-sectoral, multi-focal and multi-disciplinary nature of youth services
- appropriate training for key staff
- adequate systems of supervision and support for staff
- organisational guidelines/protocols on confidentiality, supervision and training
- comprehensive assessment of the young person
- interventions that are targeted in ways that recognise young people's developmental pattern and

assessment of their particular risk
- interventions that are able to cope with multiple individual problems
- proper communication and effective co-ordination between agencies and mechanisms for creating integrated programmes of care.

References :
Recent published documents that were discussed within this seminar were the NHS Health Advisory Report, 'Children and Young People Substance Misuse Services - the substance of young needs', the Effectiveness Task Force Report, 'Alcohol and the Young' and 'Tackling Drugs Together'.

ADAPTING TRADITIONAL SERVICES TO MEET YOUNGER NEEDS
Geoff Dalley, Area Manager, Turning Point

What is a young person? There needs to be clarity on this. If, as some do, you say a young person is someone under 25, then all the drug services I manage are doing very well at reaching this age group. However, if you are talking about the under 16s then only two of the six services I manage are doing any work with young people. This may seem basic, but there is no general agreement here, and even our funders seem not to know what they mean by *a young person*.

Most current drug services are set up for opiate users, combining detoxification and rehabilitation with needle exchanges and prescribing services. The medical model of working with drug users has little or nothing to offer stimulant users. In quoting a speaker at the LGDF Effectiveness Review Conference, who said "the best I can do for crack users is to wait until they start using heroin and then prescribe methadone", I think I am repeating something with the ring of truth, especially if all you feel you can offer is medication. Alternative therapies do seem to help stimulant users and some services are saying that they are having some success in this area of work.

There are problems with mixing services for older users with those for younger users and those available for young people are often patchy and rather on the fringe of the drug field. The one successful peer education scheme I have is funded in a very piece-meal way and is by no means secure. We have just lost funding for a *diversion from crime* scheme and, although the door is still open for future funding, we will then have the up-hill job of re-launching the scheme.

In looking at young people's drug use I would make the following points:

- Why can't *drug peer education programmes* include alcohol? The ones I am aware of teach young people about drugs, drug use and safer sex practice, but little else. I feel these services could, and should, expand their remit.
- Most young drug users do not see that *they* have a problem and will not therefore respond to the offer of drug services.
- Current drug services are based in problem areas whereas young people's use is far more wide-spread. This means not just targeting the council estate, with its more open problems, but also the respectable parts of town; in fact, the whole of the country. But are there enough drug workers to go around and who will fund this expansion?

Young people need information/education on all drugs to enable them to make informed choices about their possible drug use. Some will lose control of their drug use and will need the support and help of drug services. Most of the presenting problems will be the same problems as older drug users have and the same sort of services will be needed, but the services will have to look different to appeal to younger users.

What services will be needed?
Education
- The school programme is an 11-year one and it will be a very long time before the full impact can be seen. One problem is that the programme does not look at the issues from any ethnic points of view.
- Peer Education needs evaluation. Good ideas and good practice need to be shared. Such schemes should be expanded to include alcohol, human sexuality, group work and other issues that affect young people. They could be developed to include a NVQ or another qualification, thus making them more attractive to young people wishing to participate.
- Advice and information services, information cards etc. do exist; some are being evaluated and information could be shared.
- Outreach/detached work provides some good models, but they are only really useful in areas where there is a noticeable problem.

Recreational drug use
- Work has started within some venues such as clubs and raves with venue staff receiving training. Some venues now have a paramedic on the premises. This could be a big step forward in directing

young people experiencing problems to services and support. Some Peer Education projects go into clubs and raves and one even works with the police at a venue, as part of an arrest referral scheme.

Crack users
- They request detoxification and have money problems, yet crack is not addictive in medical terms and we cannot give them money. People talk about safe houses, but I feel this approach will not work; dealers owed large amounts of money will soon know the addresses of any safe house.
- Further research into what works would be useful; for some stimulant users relaxation and alternative therapies can be helpful.

Young people who inject
- Young people who inject will need the same services as other injecting users, but there are issues involving under 16s because of the Gillick ruling. We await a court case in relation to needle exchange and the under 16s.

Issues
- Funding: I hear two things from funders; one, work with young people and two, cuts in funding. If you put these two things together, it can only mean that we stop working with older users and focus on young people. If we receive new money, new projects could be developed along the lines of existing models. If we do not receive new money , as is most likely, we run the risk of stretching services until they crack. One way to square this circle, would be to work with other agencies and train their staff to do some of the work.
- We need more research into the needs of young drug users and what actually works. Present research has focused on school attenders, ignoring those truanting and excluded.
- How do you reach young people in rural areas? How do you cover the large areas involved?
- How do drug agencies de-mystify drugs? Young people come into contact with many agencies and their staff could have a large part to play in this work.

There are more questions than answers but some good work is happening and, given the right lead, services can adapt. The future could look bleak for some existing services, but those that change to meet the new focus on young people will survive and some will even grow.

STEPPING STONES - A DERBYSHIRE APPROACH TO DRUGS EDUCATION

David Hartwell, Derbyshire Education Authority

The Stepping Stones approaches to drugs education that have been devised in Derbyshire are the result of a two year project funded by North Derbyshire Health and Southern Derbyshire Health. The project was managed by Derbyshire County Council Education Department, Advisory and Inspection Service. The aims of the project were:

- To focus on young people aged 11-16
- To target those young people who resist schooling and thereby are at special risk of not gaining any drugs education
- To develop strategies to provide the target group with drugs education

The outcome of this project may be recognised as a set of stepping stones, each providing a reference point that creates an awareness of how drugs education aimed at disaffected young people may be approached.

Stepping Stone A
Attributes of disaffected young people. Material from two documents provide some background.

Dealing with Disaffection   Tim Pickles 1992
- Disaffection tends to occur only where young people are not participating within an organisation of their own free will.
- Without a sense of ownership and belonging in an organisation, risk of disaffection is increased.
- Our non co-operation arises in a situation where we do not have free choice in our actions.
- Disruptive behaviour, noncompliance with rules, minimal effort and opting out are all ways of asserting independence where conformity is expected.
- Disaffected young people are unlikely to regard present circumstances as a consequence of their own actions, feel relatively powerless to change the situation, and are alienated from 'conventional' norms. They assert independence and power through other actions.

Drugs Education for Young Offenders   TACADE 1994
Robert Ross's Canadian programme, Reason and Rehabilitation (1991)
- Empirical work indicates delayed development of cognitive skills, which are essential for social competence. Not all are poor thinkers, some think well even too well!
- Adolescent offenders and substance abusers are most likely to have cognitive defects such as
    - failing to stop and think before acting
    - difficulty in understanding reason
    - inflexibility
    - poor problem solving
    - lack of sensitivity
    - values... if it's good for me, it's good
    - poor critical reasoning (illogical)
- A number of studies have established that many young offenders are deficient in life skills, and that in turn may increase the likelihood of drug misuse.

Stepping Stone   B
It has become generally recognised that for a drugs education programme to be effective, the curriculum needs to include the following key aspects.

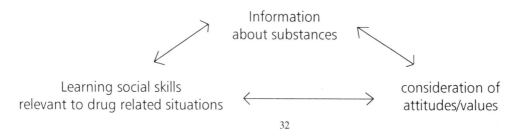

Stepping Stone C

If the attributes of disaffected young people are viewed alongside the drugs education curriculum it is reasonable to conclude that educational activity that has a primary focus on social skills should form a substantial proportion of drugs education with this target group. To increase the chances of engaging disaffected young people in any learning experience on offer, educational activity needs to acknowledge certain principles. These principles are:

- The learning activity needs to **attract** participants.
- Participants need to feel **involved** through the use of images and literature they relate to.
- There needs to be **equality** between participant and educator, achieved by all parties sharing in the gathering of information and generating knowledge.
- Information gathered and knowledge generated needs to be **owned** by the participants.
- A feeling of **achievement** needs to be gained through the completion of tasks at a variety of levels in the learning process.

Stepping Stone D

To deliver a drugs education programme with disaffected young people who require an approach which acknowledges their need for feelings of equality, ownership and achievement, there are certain variables that should be considered. These are:

- The educational **resource material** used
- The **skills of the educator**
- The **setting** where the learning experience takes place

Are each of these adequate and appropriate ?

It has been found that the setting proved to be of greater significance than is often realised in attempting drugs education with disaffected young people.

Three general types of setting are acknowledged. These are

Directed activity groups	**Closed groups**	**Non directed activity groups**
e.g. school classroom	e.g. social work therapy	e.g. general youth club gathering

It is necessary to consider the educational setting to be used with a view to recognise the implications for the level of equality, ownership and achievement that can be reached.

Stepping Stone E

At this point there should be an acknowledgement of certain key points.   step

- The attributes of disaffected young people require social skills to be a primary focus
  within the drugs education curriculum.   A/B
- The educational resources used and the learning experience devised need to take
  account of equality, ownership and achievement in order to attract and involve
  participants.   C
- There are implications for the setting in which participants are brought together that
  will affect the level of ownership, equality and empowerment they feel.   D

The Stepping Stones project devised a range of resource materials that
- rely on cartoon images rather than text
- make use of large tactile materials
- create tasks that require groups to interact and achieve the formulation of materials upon which a variety of questions may be triggered.

The resource materials form sets of games/activities. Each of these are designed to attract participants, provide opportunities for social interaction, provide an achievable task which they own and become a trigger for a variety of drug related questions and challenges to be discussed.

THE POLICE PERSPECTIVE

Keith Hellawell QPM, Chief Constable, West Yorkshire Police

I joined the police service about thirty five years ago. In those days you did six weeks on nights to learn the beats. Within the first week I found a man lying on the pavement who was blind drunk. We had no personal radios, so I went to the Doctor Who box and rang in and said, 'I've found a man drunk, what do I do with him?' 'We'll send the van out.' The black maria came out, we bundled this man into the van, took him to the police station, he was charged and put in the cells. He was taken to court and because he was a persistent drunk he ended up in prison. About three months later I saw the same drunk on the pavement in the same state. I felt as a young police officer: What value is there in dealing with this man in this way? It isn't affecting his behaviour, it's cluttering up the courts, we had to disinfect and clean out the police station, and the van, for obvious reasons. Really it was a cycle that was never ending.

Thankfully now we deal with drunks in a different way; we have detoxification centres. We have very few drunks going through the courts and ending up in prison. Today we believe that the criminal justice system is inappropriate for people who have an alcoholic problem. I think without a great deal of intellect you can see where this argument is taking me. It probably took twenty five years to change attitudes and minds, to deal with people with drink problems in a different way. My question in relation to drugs is: why not adopt the philosophy that it took us twenty or thirty years to develop in relation to alcohol? We are seeing, as you know, thousands upon thousands of young people going through the courts after being arrested not for being drug addicts but for committing minor crime to feed a drug habit. We are arresting them, and putting them before a court, and into a criminal justice system that is not geared up to deal with them. They go through the system eventually ending up in prison, come out of prison, commit crime, go back into the system. I know we're trying, but we're not having any substantial success in breaking that cycle.

I think when I first talked in this way, and I have been doing so now, for probably ten years, people regarded me as some sort of liberal Chief Constable who had lost his head. But when the modern police service, as we call it, was set up more than 150 years ago, the first principle on which it was formed was the prevention of crime. Then there was the protection of the public, the safety of the public and last the prosecution of offenders. We were set up to prevent crime. When I take a look at the police service - and it's getting better - the amount of resources, and time and energy we devote to preventing crime is very small compared to the amount of time we spend on detecting and dealing with those who have committed crime. So I think we have a substantial way to go with Drug Action Teams, in terms of diversion, in terms of treatment and in terms of other enlightened ways of dealing with people who commit crime because of drugs.

I went to Cambridge University in 1970. I was a Detective Inspector at that time, and the first paper I was asked to write was about the police service. Was the police service an enforcement agency or an adjunct to the social services? It was an interesting question in 1970 and it is an interesting question today. I feel that among all the agencies represented here today there is still perhaps some concern , unease or lack of clarity about where we all stand in dealing with the social issues that are facing us. I understand from the groups that there have been concerns about the police involvement in DATs. They do not get involved at the right level or do not have the right commitment. But we all, because of the pressures under which we operate, have our own primary focus. For a voluntary agency, the primary focus, sad as it might sound, could well be on survival. Maybe the involvement of a statutory agency like the police service could be seen as a threat to its very existence.

I think there is a second problem apart from that arena of expertise and professionalism and territorial independence. We all think we know best - we have been trained, we understand it more than anyone else. I think if we are honest, we are all, to a degree, guilty of that. How many times have we, each of us, gone into meetings, believing that we know as much if not more than other agencies there, and have expressed internally, sometimes externally, the frustration at the lack of knowledge or lack of understanding of others?

But as a group we are facing some of the most complex, sophisticated social problems that our society has ever faced. We still do not know everything about the subject we are trying to deal with. As some of you know, I have been calling for a long time for a national research centre. We have not yet got a firm basis upon which we can decide what are the real issues, the real problems, and the solutions we want. In many instances we think, well, this is going to work, this looks good, we've heard that may work but there is no body of knowledge to show that any particular type of community service would operate well or that it will achieve the desired outcomes.

We come from different backgrounds, we view things in different ways and therefore I think it is not surprising that there are tensions between us, not just in terms of publicity or in terms of language but in terms of DATs and other groupings when we come together. We are trying to resolve some very, very complex, sophisticated issues. If I felt that the police alone could resolve the problem, I would say leave it to us. Or if education could, or social services, or probation, the health service, voluntary agencies, parents or teachers. But we all know that no one single agency, no one single body could resolve this problem within our midst. And it isn't as if there were a single problem. There is the problem of the thirteen or fourteen year old girl or fifteen year old boy who is the victim of prostitution, the victim of males largely who will prey upon them, who will buy their bodies because the children are addicted to drugs. And that is a totally different problem to the seventeen or eighteen year old who goes out on a Saturday night and takes Ecstasy. And he or she is in a totally different league to the cannabis taker who probably causes no one any trouble and who certainly does not cause disruption on the street, although they may be a danger on the roads, or in the work place, and they may be in some other danger through taking that drug.

We are facing several different, complex problems. We all have our own agendas, visions, messages, and causes, and all bring a great deal of energy and dynamism. But we must realise that we cannot resolve all the problems and all the issues that we are facing at one or two moves. I think we have got a very positive basis. I believe that there is a willingness to get round the table together and to look for a common agenda, and common goals and outcomes. Given the multiplicity of agencies and backgrounds, this is in itself a substantial achievement, and it is a start.

The press ask me, are these problems going to be resolved? Will we stop drugs by the end of the century? I think everyone here realises that is a pipe dream. We need to look at what can be tolerated. We need to help people who need helping. We need a criminal justice system that takes account of the problems and issues associated with drug taking by young people particularly addiction. We also need links between all those services. As Roger Howard says (see page 8), it cannot be solved just at Drug Action Team level. I think it must be at government level. Government controls the major departments of state that bid for money, and operate as separate entities and when it comes down to us at local level we are then asked to co-operate. I think we could give a much stronger message if we had more of a corporate approach. To be fair to government, the White Paper contained the beginning of that corporate approach.

I have not mentioned drugs courts because it follows from what I have said, that drugs courts will not be enough. I agree with Roger Howard that we cannot just take something off the shelf from America. We can take the principles, but I think the principle of the drugs court implies that the criminal justice system as it was in America does not cope adequately, and does not start to resolve the issues associated with addiction by young people. We can look at the idea behind drugs courts rather than saying we need to copy them as they stand.

Can I as Chief Constable, thank all of you for the work that you do. Without people who care, the situation could be a whole lot worse than it is.

DRUGS: THE PROBATION RESPONSE

Paul Hayes, ACPO, S.E. London Probation Service

I shall talk about tackling drugs and offending together because that's what the probation service has to do in relation to drug misuse and offending: tackle the two together. What I want to do first of all is ask what's all this got to do with the probation service? Second and also within that, why should drug services, and other people involved in this, be interested in what the probation service is doing? And then what, should probation managers be doing?

Before that I want to spend a couple of minutes reflecting on what Howard Parker said (see page 19). Several points I found very interesting. The first is the normalisation of drugs issue. When we are talking about offenders, we are talking about a group that have selected themselves out of normality, so the people the Prison Service is dealing with, the people that most drugs services are dealing with, the people the probation service is dealing with, are the casualties of normal drug use, just as the alcohol misuse problems that we deal with, are the casualities of normal alcohol use. So to say drug use does not lead to crime, as Howard Parker does, is absolutely true, but drug use and crime are linked, and they are linked very closely. And what the probation service and other agencies need to do is understand that link.

The next thing really is something I'd like to take issue with. He is a bit critical of *Tackling Drugs Together* and particularly of the link between drugs and crime. Those of us who actually have to deliver services recognise how you have to package things together in order to make them politically attractive. In this context the link between crime, youth and drugs is probably very helpful. Drug services were driven by public health and HIV for many years. As that panic, not the problem but the panic, receded, another driver was needed in order to justify the government expenditure of public money on drug misuse. Another driver of course is the background concern. Nice middle class girls at safe campus universities might use drugs so their parents who are in positions of power justify the expenditure on drug services. But it is crime, the fear of crime , the perceived link between drug use and crime that gives drug misuse, the whole drug misuse strategy, political leverage. Without that I suspect the whole thing would not have anything like the priority it has been given and what follows from that is that the efforts that many of us are engaged in to deal with drug misuse wouldn't actually be possible because the resources wouldn't be there.

Why is the probation service involved in working with drug misuse?

First of all the probation service's primary task is to understand the relationship between people's behaviour and crime. In particular, to understand the relationship between drug use and crime in order to reduce crime, and hopefully to prevent crime from occurring at all. It's easy to condemn crime. If you've actually got to do something about it to stop it, you've got to understand what's going on. What is the precise relationship between this individual and this substance and their anti-social behaviour? The probation service has a unique role in the criminal justice system. Police officers see something going on, they see someone who they think has done it, and they nick them. They aren't particularly bothered about the causality, they're not that interested in what's gone on behind that offence, what actually triggered it. The courts are interested in evidence; is there enough evidence to say this person did it? The Prison Service to some extent are interested in what's going on behind this behaviour, in order to influence it. But increasingly now, they're much more interested in making sure the person stays where they've been put. The probation service is the bit of the criminal justice system that is charged with the responsibility, first of all, of informing courts what is going on for people, what is actually happening, through pre-sentence reports. Why is this person doing the things they're doing? And secondly, understanding that link, actually taking some action whilst they're under community sentence or following release from prison, to make it less likely to happen again.

The second thing is scale; study after study has shown something like 25/30% of the probation service's case load seriously misuses drugs. That does not mean people having the odd spliff of cannabis, the recreational drug use Howard Parker describes. It's people who are committing burglaries to sustain serious cocaine and heroin habits; it's people who get smashed out of their heads on designer lager and amphetamines, and then wreck night clubs, or smash people over the head with bottles. Or it's people who want to sustain a lifestyle that involves spending £70-80 on a Friday or Saturday night doing that and can't get a job. They want to sustain that life style and all the things that go with it, this week's shirt or getting into the right clubs, wearing the right trainers, all that goes along with the whole consumer concept that Howard talks about, but they can't keep up with other people because they have been excluded from legitimate sources of income. So the probation service cannot afford to ignore this work.

Neither can we afford to contract it out. There are some forty to fifty thousand people who misuse drugs in contact with probation officers in any one day. That's not a throughput figure, its a snapshot figure: forty or fifty thousand people. We can't contract that out because firstly we'd all be out of a job if we did. Secondly I don't know who'd take them on. So the scale of it means it's a business we've got to stay in. Thirdly the probation service is involved at every stage of the process: cautioning, bail decisions, pre-sentence reports, community sentences, through-care, supervising people on licence. We've even got the odd probation officer left in the odd prison somewhere in the country. That's not entirely a flippant point; one of the key points made in the ACMD report on prisons is the crucial role of through and after care, the transition from prison back into the community. The assumption is made throughout all of that that the role of the probation service in achieving that link will be crucial. Who will fulfil that role if POs are no longer in prisons?

Finally this is a 'Hard to Reach' population. Everybody knows that the people actually accessing drugs services are overwhelmingly white, in their late twenties to early thirties, and male. The probation service, because of the operation of the criminal justice system, scoops up very large numbers of young drug users who would not be accessing services in any other way; black drug users and women drug users who would have more difficulty accessing services otherwise. For example, in one probation service, on any one day, the probation officers will be in contact with six hundred people who misuse drugs aged under twenty one, seven hundred and fifty black drug misusers and over six hundred women drug misusers. Only 1 in 5 of those will be in contact with any other drug service. So therefore it is vital for the probation service to be involved in this business and it is vital for other people to be working alongside the probation service if they want to access those client groups.

The Probation Service Strategy

So what's the strategy? The strategy as set out by the Home Office in its guidance to the probation services is that every service ought to have a policy, ought to be involved in partnerships in order to gather information, in order to train staff, and to promote good practice. And all this needs to be informed by good anti-discriminatory practice. So what does that mean in some detail?

First of all you need a policy which **legitimises current practice**, which enables probation officers to work to reduce harm, not always to produce abstinence. Now that's quite complex in a criminal justice context. If someone discloses that they are using an illegal substance, they are telling you they are committing an offence. The probation service could very easily get rid of all its drug misusing clients overnight by saying 'if you tell me you're using you'll be nicked' and all of a sudden we wouldn't have any. So if we're actually going to deal with people effectively, to tackle their drug use and their offending, we need to encourage them to come forward: we need a policy which enables probation officers to feel safe in working with people who are disclosing drug use and disclosing how it interacts with their offending. The Home Office have actually endorsed that approach in a Home Office circular. The Association of Chief Officers of Probation supported that, and every probation service in the country is now being expected, within the *'Tackling Drugs Together'* strategy, to draw up a policy which legitimises practice which in fact has been going on since the development of original harm reduction practices. Services such as Merseyside have been practising like this for twelve or thirteen years now.

Secondly, **Partnership**. Probation officers have the skills, resources and opportunities to work effectively with drug misusers. Drug misusers, we are now all taught to believe, exercise rational choice about their behaviour. Given that, then the skills the probation officers use every day in their work to engage with offenders are equally applicable in their work with drug misusers. But we can't do it all. We can't detox people, we can't prescribe, we can't necessarily give them enough time. A criminal justice agency is not necessarily the right atmosphere in which to be doing those things. We haven't always got all the expertise we need. No, we need to draw on other agencies. We need to draw on their resources and their skills. It isn't a matter of either/or, the probation officer or the other agency. Probation officers need to identify what bits they can do, what bits other people can do and what bits need to be dealt with together.

Information. It's vital that we actually know what's going on. We need to gather basic information about how many people are using, what they are using, how are they using, how they are getting it and so forth. That's important not only to inform our practice, because we're dealing with such large numbers of people. Other people's practice and strategies need to be informed by what we're doing. Probation information needs to be incorporated in a drug misuse database in order for people such as DATs to be able to plan their activities more effectively.

Training. We need to skill up our own staff to do this work. Some probation officers are absolutely excellent at working with drug misusers, some are hopeless, most are in the middle. We need to either skill up or get rid of the hopeless ones, improve the ones in the middle, so that they come up to the competency of the best and enable the best to become even better in order to drag standards forward.

Finally **anti-discriminatory practice**. Drug misusers are a marginalised, discriminated-against group anyway. It's even more problematic if you're black and a drug misuser. There are all sorts of assumptions about drug use amongst black communities. If you are a single mother and a drug user you can have concerns about what's going to happen to your children, so it is vital that the approaches that the probation service adopts take into account the additional burdens that people are going to experience as well as the fact that you are dealing with a stigmatized group in any event. Let's now look at practice in a little more detail.

Best practice

So what is best practice supposed to look like? First of all we should be promoting disclosure. If you are going to work with someone to change their behaviour, then it needs to be a co-operative and dynamic situation not a one-off. People change, they use different substances at different times, their patterns of behaviour change, they start, they stop. The classic scenario a probation officer would face would be somebody who is appearing in court on a string of burglaries, who would work their ticket by saying 'It wasn't me guv, it was the heroin'. The first time they report to the office, they say to the probation officer 'I've knocked it on the head now, I'm not doing it'. So you've had disclosure but there's nowhere you can go with it. The process needs to be continuing, the person needs to actually be prepared to say what's going on. Obviously that's vital when you come to things like relapse, but it's important even if you are assessing the situation to know which particular substances they are using and in what ways. You need something which is an honest process.

Secondly the **drug/crime link**. The relationship between drugs and crime is complex. It isn't one dimensional, not simply that you are dependent on heroin or crack cocaine therefore you have to go out and commit a string of burglaries. The probability is that most people who misuse drugs do not start committing offences, other than by virtue of breaching the Misuse of Drugs Act. Drugs don't cause criminals, but they very probably do cause crime, because people who would be involved in crime in any event become involved in more crime, more often and their criminal career probably lasts longer. It seems to me therefore that it's very important for us to understand the variety of ways in which drug misuse and crime can interact. Someone who is committing burglaries linked with a serious heroin habit is behaving in very different ways to someone who's getting smashed out of their heads on a Saturday night and committing criminal damage or someone who is driving round the streets of Liverpool or Manchester with a machine gun, actually controlling access to a drug market. Those three behaviours are very different: to call them all drug related crime is to risk confusion.

The next thing really is to **build motivation**. We used to believe that you used to have to sit there and wait for people to get motivated. Not alot of them did. Most people use drugs because they enjoy it; they continue using drugs while they enjoy it. There's a downside to using drugs; the downside for a lot of people will involve offending. If it involves offending it will mean getting nicked. If you're getting nicked then you begin to think. At first, it's a bit of a laugh, you're seventeen or eighteen, all your mates are getting nicked, so what? You start growing up a bit, you start getting sentenced. You start getting sentenced for things that mean something to you, six months, twelve months, eighteen months. You've picked up a partner and maybe some children along the way. All of a sudden it's not so much fun any longer. So probation officers can actually access that and begin to work with people. Is this making sense for you any longer or isn't it? Should you be doing it, or shouldn't you? What options have you got? What choices have you got? What can you do about it? What will you do next time you're in that position? in order to weigh up what's sensible for them or what isn't sensible for them. But you don't just sit there and wait until 'Oh well I've decided to stop now'. You actually start accessing those things, widening those cracks at the earliest possible time, trying to emphasise the down side for them, trying to get them to put the good bits into perspective, often giving them an excuse to start thinking about coming off.

The next thing is to **support and sustain change**. If you've been doing something for years it's very difficult to stop, particularly if you've got very little else in your life. So it's not just working with people's drug misuse. It's also working with their housing, their employment, access to education, the relationships they've got with other people, in order to support and sustain the change.

It's vital to use **partner agencies**. As I've said before, the probation service can't do it all. We need to use other people in order to bring their expertise to bear. We've got to expect relapse. Just as we do with every other offender it gives you an opportunity actually to look at what's going on, what stage you've really achieved, what's actually happening for the person in order to build on that. You've got to expect three steps forward and two back, sometimes two forward and three back, and try and try again.

Finally, and this is where some of us might part company, **enforcement**. This is still going on within a criminal justice enforced relationship. The person has been sentenced by a court or they have been released from a prison with the understanding that they have got certain obligations. Now if we believe that drug users are rational people capable of exercising choice about their behaviour, which we've all been telling everybody else for the last ten years, it seems very difficult for us to believe that they cease to be able to exercise choice about that either when they offend or when obligations are placed on them by a court. If they can turn up to get their script, if they can sign on, if they can meet their dealer, if they can meet the mates that they commit offences with, then they can keep to the obligations of their supervision. Probation officers have to enforce court orders within a framework of national standards and there is or should be no particular reason why drug misusers should be exempted from those standards.

So that's what we're supposed to be doing, that's the framework that's set out, for policy and for practice. What I want to talk about now is where we've got to with that, what's really going on.

Progress to date

The Home Office is currently inspecting the probation service's work with drug misusers. The first inspection will be looking at probation services' policies and the second will be looking at practice. The inspection into policies is just about to be completed and will be reporting back next week or the week after. Every service has got a policy: whether they all match a template that was issued by the Home Office is another matter, but they all exist. The probability is that not all of them will be as expected by the Home Office. That's one of the themes of this section of the presentation: patchiness. Just as with practice the best is excellent, the worst is way below standard and most will just bump along in the middle. The objective, of course, is to bring everybody up to at least the competent and hopefully towards the level of the best.

Because of the difficulty faced by criminal justice agencies actually working with people who were acknowledging they were continuing to offend, some probation services, particularly probation committees, the judges and magistrates who are the legal authority for the service, found it very difficult to explicitly endorse harm reduction practice. That's why it was thought helpful to have guidance from the Home Office to support it. Now that that's come out, all services have actually developed policies.

Partnership. Probation services are increasingly becoming involved in partnerships with other agencies. Probation services are active in DATs, but the effectiveness of DATs is very variable indeed. I suspect that in some places the probation service and the other criminal justice agencies need to improve their input into DATs. We are doing something about that within ACOP in order to try to foster probation service involvement.

As many of you will know a target was set for the probation services that 5% of their expenditure should be spent in partnership with the voluntary sector. An awful lot of probation services were prevented from spending that on drug services because their local drug service providers were NHS. That structure is now probably going to break down. The Home Office has now done an inspection on the partnership process and has discovered it was actually delivering very poor value for money in many ways. The 5% was needed to kick start services. I think it's probable that the restrictions on investing in NHS services will also be relaxed, maybe not immediately but certainly quite soon, in order to facilitate funding through the DATs.

Community Care. Again, variable. In some places the probation service is very actively involved with social services and health authorities. In other places, the probation services don't want to know. And in some other places probation services are banging on the door and no one will let them in. But I think the probation service is coming to view its responsibilities much more clearly as regards community safety. And increasingly the police are reaching out to the population as a whole and seeing crime prevention as one of their key functions. I think a situation is developing whereby police and probation service can co-operate far more effectively than they have in the past.

Information. A lot of progress has been made on information. We've got a new computer system coming in, on which drug information will be integrated. Some probation services, Suffolk for example, have moved forward and are producing very interesting sophisticated detailed data on all offenders and that is being used as a template for many other services.

Training. Three years ago the Home Office commissioned from NACRO a pack to use with probation officers in order to skill up probation officers to work more effectively with drug and alcohol misuse. That should be coming out this year and should provide services not only with the framework within which to train staff but also with useful training materials which reflect the particular concerns the probation service faces.

The second element of the inspection relates to practice. At the moment you know as much as I do about how effective probation service practice is. I think it would be futile of me to speculate on what will emerge from that inspection. I know it won't all be good news. There's no point in having an inspectorate if it only tells you good news. I hope there's enough good news in it for us to build on. There's every reason to believe there is but when that report comes out next year probably we'll then at least then have an idea what we need to do in order to have practice that more nearly matches the ideal.

DRUG USE IN PRISON: THE CURRENT PICTURE

Dr Libby Joyce , Directorate of Health Care, HM Prison Service

SUMMARY

The 1980's brought to the United Kingdom increasing awareness of the escalation of drug misuse both in the community and within the prison system, heightened by recognition of the implications that this might have for the spread of HIV infection. As the eighties ended, there was increasing, justified criticism that responses to this threat were inadequate: education, treatment and rehabilitation services were in very short supply, particularly for those in custody, and were characterised by lack of coordination and liaison between the various agencies and services involved with misusers of drugs before, during and after imprisonment. Data on the numbers and characteristics of those using drugs, on patterns of misuse and use of services, were lacking for both prisoners and the community.

The early 90's saw greatly increased activity on all fronts, fuelled by encouraging reports from abroad - particularly the USA - of success in treatment and rehabilitation programmes. Key research on prisoners and in the community uncovered the scale and evolution of drugs misuse particularly in the young. It confirmed that:

- a higher proportion of those entering prison than of the general population have a history of misuse of drugs (including alcohol) and a higher percentage will have used opiates and have injected drugs
- age is a key factor in both the numbers using illicit drugs and the types of drugs being used. The majority of young men in the population have used illicit drugs at some time and the proportion using heroin and cocaine increases in the twenties age group.

However, studies have shown that the number using drugs while in prison is less than those entering with a history of misuse and that injecting behaviour is reduced when in prison. There is no evidence to indicate that this effect is continued on return to the community, and the small numbers who misuse drugs for the first time when they are in prison add to those who continue during their time in custody, and who probably will continue when released unless there has been successful intervention.

The Prison Service has the task of reducing the damage to the individual, to the prison community and to society that drug misuse brings, by creating an environment where the decrease in illegal drug use is the maximum possible and is likely to continue on release back to the community. Great strides have been made, with an integrated strategy which attacks both the supply of drugs to prisoners and their demand for them and seeks to limit the damage and risk caused by misuse of drugs. This strategy is based on extensive research into the experience of other countries in both control and treatment initiatives in prisons, and all new programmes and control measures will be subject to extensive independent evaluation as well as internal monitoring. Shifts in the patterns, as well as the extent, of misuse within the prison system will be carefully assessed.

The prison system is not responsible for the escalation of illicit drug use in society, nor can it eradicate it. However, it has a unique opportunity to create an environment where availability is minimal and access to appropriate help and support is maximal. Achievement of this ideal will be much more difficult, and will lose its point, if the world outside the prison system remains the same and fails to support those emerging from prisons who have managed to effect personal change. The Government's comprehensive strategy "Tackling Drugs Together" embraces the Prison Service's strategy. The dominant theme is concerted action - liaison and collaboration across the prison walls and across agency walls. The good news is that this is happening now, and we must secure it, increase it and improve it in the years ahead.

I. BACKGROUND

I am indebted to Professor David Smith of Lancaster University for the following elegant summary of the recent history of therapeutic endeavour within the custodial system:

1960 - 70's	:	naive optimism
1970 - 80's	:	naive pessimism
1980 - 90's	:	cautious, rational, (informed) optimism

In relation to therapy specifically for drug (and alcohol) misuse, the first stage is perhaps least applicable. However, my experience as a medical practitioner in the 80's would certainly support the contention that there was a great deal of pessimism regarding the potential for cure of what were seen as the intractable, chronic and relapsing diseases of alcoholism and drug addiction. That the narrow medical model of treatment and rehabilitation, which in many places was all that was on offer, had severe limitations became increasingly clear as the eighties progressed. The gradual seeding of more accessible services in the community, which employed a wider range of approaches and techniques - including "shopfronts" - and involved many more disciplines and agencies, was the true start of a more optimistic response.

Warning shots concerning the escalation of problem drug misuse had been fired in the 60's, but it was during the 70's that increasing awareness of the impact on society and in prisons started to emerge. An early and important reaction was the creation of the Advisory Council on the Misuse of Drugs (ACMD) in 1971. This statutory body, formed of independent experts, is responsible for continual review of illegal drugs and drugs subject to misuse in society and for reporting their findings to Government. A sub group - The Criminal Justice Working Group - was formed in 1990 and I would recommend its third report, "Drugs Misusers and the Prison System - An Integrated Approach,"[1] to all interested in this subject.

Alongside the increase in community programmes, the 80's brought increasing attempts to describe and quantify the problem - both through analyses of routinely collected data and research studies. The increase in notifications of registered drug addicts to the Home Office since the beginning of the 90's is demonstrated in Figure 1, with separate curves for total notifications for England and Wales and for notifications from prisons. Prisoners have contributed an increasing percentage of these notifications rising from 12% in 1990 to 23% in 1994/5 and a further increase is predicted in data for 1995/6.

In addition to routine notification of registered addicts, the Prison Service started in 1994 to record numbers of others diagnosed as addicted to drugs but not registered, who were identified by prison health care centres. There were over 5,000 recorded in 1994/5 and this is expected to increase substantially for 1995/6. Both figures (prison notifications and recording of non-notifiable addicts) however, are liable to double-counting as prisoners leave and then re-enter the system within the same year.

Figure 1

Number of Notifiable Drug Addicts in England and Wales

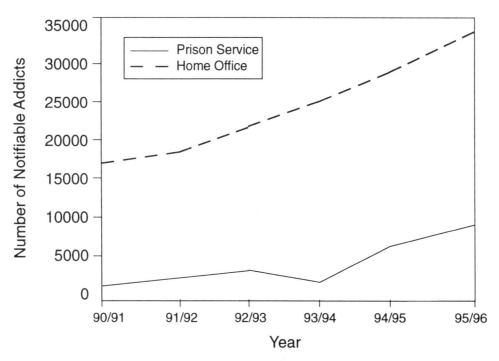

With the exception of a guidance note issued by the Prison Service in 1984, which encouraged awareness and response by health care staff, services within the prison setting were slow to follow the movement to diversified services in the community outside, and this led to both justifiable criticism and useful recommendations.

The 1991 Report "Mentally Disordered Prisoners,"[2] (Gunn, Maden and Swinton) reported the following observations from their 1989/90 research into psychiatric morbidity in sentenced prisoners:

- Drug dependence is the most common psychiatric problem in sentenced prisoners
- The main result of concern about drug abuse is to prevent it within the prison: most staff assume that inmates will return to drug abuse when they leave prison
- With rare exceptions, prison doctors regarded drug and alcohol abuse as being outside their area of concern
- There was a complete lack of familiarity with local facilities for helping drug users, and with current approaches to treatment.

This was the first national study to provide insight into the extent and characteristics of drug misuse by prisoners in England.

As well as criticism of the lack of service provided in response to the needs of drugs misusers coming into prison, there were many who remarked on the adverse characteristics of prison culture. As Professor Martin Plant comments in his review of studies of therapeutic programmes in prison[3]: "the inherently non-therapeutic environment of prisons serves to limit the effectiveness of both drug abuse treatment and AIDS education provided within prisons". He also notes that the culture tends to support the illicit use of drugs and that "imprisonment may increase rather than reduce the likelihood that an individual will continue to use drugs".

However, I hope to show in the following sections that it is possible to change this adverse culture with the active will of prisoners and staff - and I commend particularly the review by Player and Martin of the ADT programme at Downview[4], on this topic. I will also use the results of some recent studies to show that fewer prisoners who use drugs in the community do so in prison and, although there is a small proportion who use illicit drugs for the first time in prison, there is still a net decrease in illicit use within prisons.

Finally in this section I have turned to Professor Gunn's seminal study again (op cit), to provide summaries of some key recommendations to the Prison Service, which helped to shape its way forward. The themes contained in these recommendations have been reiterated in most subsequent literature on the subject.

Among the recommendations were the requirements to:

- address the need for a policy, for improved training and for services within prisons
- introduce a standard opiate withdrawal regime
- provide access to education, individual and group counselling and therapeutic communities
- provide preparation for release
- establish two-way contact with outside agencies.

These recommendations, made in 1991, have been at the heart of our evolving Prison Service strategy for drug misuse in prisons and great strides have been made towards their achievement.

II. SIZE, CHARACTERISTICS AND TRENDS

I would like to review briefly the results of some major studies which have contributed significantly to our understanding of the extent and nature of drug misuse by prisoners, and also briefly refer to work which has underpinned the strategic response by the Prison Service in its development of therapeutic services.

However, I must first admit some major limitations of this review.

1. Work on the population of female prisoners is excluded. Not because this is less important - except in numbers, as they constitute less than 4% of the prison population - but because the prevalence and pattern of drugs misuse in the female population is substantially different from that of the male population and would necessarily entail separate treatment of each of the points. Space, unfortunately, prohibits this. Serious attention is being given to these differences in investigating the particular needs of women drug misusers in prison and in construction of

programmes to meet their particular needs.

2. My presentation is limited to the misuse of drugs, and I have not included any parallel data on, or consideration of, alcohol misuse. The impact of alcohol misuse is of major concern and, again, its absence from this presentation does not mean lack of recognition of our need to address this form of addiction also.

3. The Report of the Government's Task Force to Review Services for Drug Misusers[5] provides a useful definition of substance misuse. "Drug misuse is used to denote drug taking which is hazardous or harmful and unsanctioned by professional or cultural standards. It is broadly equivalent to such terms as drug abuse and problem drug taking." Standards within the prison setting are, and must be, strictly according to the law and regulations of the criminal justice system. The law has recently been changed to create an offence of taking illicit drugs in prison, as determined currently by mandatory testing of urine. In this context, the taking of all substances categorised by the law as illegal, or illegal without prescription, is therefore drug misuse, and the review of data is based on this premise.

4. Finally, the following tables do not present strictly comparable values. They ignore the differences between the studies from which they come. They are presented merely as a very preliminary attempt to coordinate an ever-increasing body of data and, in doing so, to see whether there are clear indications of common trends or useful hypotheses.

Table 1 looks at various data on the prevalence of drugs misuse in the community, as estimated by studies on the general population, and studies which have asked prisoners about their drug-taking before entering prison.

Table 1
DRUG MISUSE BEFORE ENTRY

ANY DRUG OF MISUSE: adult males (16-69)

%	Period	Pop'n	n	Study	Year
20	Lifetime	General	2958	B. C. S. [6]	1992
17	Lifetime	General	4859	OPCS/Household [7]	1993/4
77.5	Lifetime	Pris: R+S	1009	IOP: HIV [8]	1994
77	Lifetime	Pris: R	750	TOP: Remand [9]	1993/4
70+	Lifetime	Pris: R+S	344	ACMD Survey [1]	1995
8	1 year	General	2958	B. C. S. [6]	1992
63	1 year	Pris: S	982	OPCS: Sentencd [10]	1994
43	6 months	Pris: S	1751	IOP:Sentenced [2]	1989/90
35	1 month	Pris: R+S	1173	Merseyside [11]	1995

Immediately noticeable is the very large difference between the proportions who admit ever having used drugs illicitly: around 20% for the general population but in the 70% range (consistently) for prisoners before entry to prison. This confirms, as all comparative studies have, that the prison population contains a much higher proportion of people who have used illicit drugs than the general community.

The second most noticeable feature is the "fall-off" effect within the prison population over time: from somewhere in the 70% range for a "lifetime, prevalence - i.e. have ever used - to 63% having used within the preceding year, to 43% within the preceding 6 months, and 34% within the preceding month. That this is associated with the decay in numbers which occurs from experimental use, to recreational use, to dependency is an obvious hypothesis. It is also noticeable that the size of "fall-off" appears much less for the prison population than for the general population.

It is likely that those most easily discouraged by a mandatory random testing scheme with incurred penalties will be those with less frequent or irregular use. However, conversely, should supply be readily available and the culture favourable, there is a large population coming into prison who, having already "experimented" may take any opportunity to experiment further, or use more regularly.

It is generally thought that the British Crime Study[6] and the Household Survey of Psychiatric Morbidity[7] findings underestimate the true extent of drug misuse in the community. Another explanation of the marked difference between the findings for use in the community and by prisoners has been the effect of age. It is true that this will contribute to the overall magnitude of the difference between the two populations, as their age profiles are different. The younger age groups are much more strongly represented in the prison population.

However, Figure 2 shows a remarkably consistent relationship between the results found for the general population and those for the prison population, as well as demonstrating the strong relationship of drug taking to age.

Figure 2

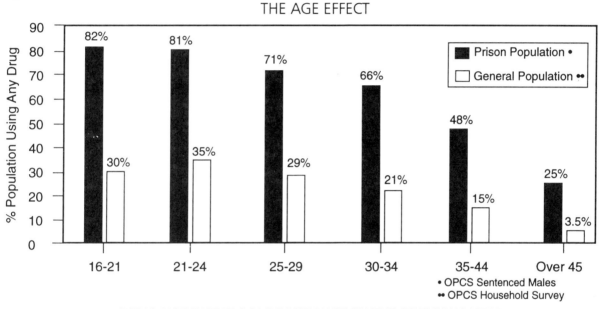

THE AGE EFFECT

DRUG USE IN THE COMMUNITY WITHIN THE PREVIOUS YEAR

The histogram blocks represent "lifetime prevalence" - i.e. answers to questions as to whether the subjects have ever used. Similar diagrams relating age to types of drug use - e.g. degree of dependency or use of different types of drugs - are likely to have rather different patterns for both the general population and the prison population. This is illustrated in the following figure.

Figure 3

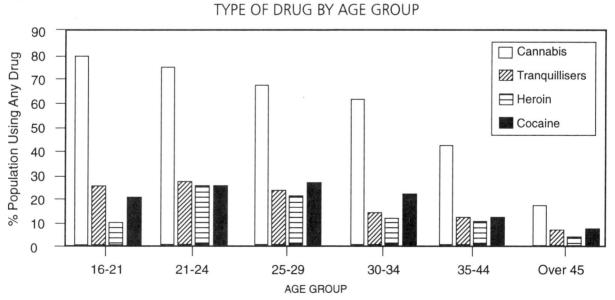

TYPE OF DRUG BY AGE GROUP

DRUG USE BY PRISONERS WITHIN ONE YEAR PRIOR TO ENTRY

Figure 3 was compiled from the results of the Office of Population Censuses and Surveys (OPCS) Survey of the Physical Health of Male Sentenced Prisoners in 1994[8] and illustrates the differences between 5-year age groups, in the proportions using four types of drug in the community during the year prior to entry to prison.

The peak age for cannabis use is under 21, followed by a steady decline. The peaks for heroin and cocaine occur later - in the twenties - and decline is somewhat slower, with the rate of decay of cocaine use lowest among these four types. Use of benzodiazepines starts earlier than heroin but follows the same decaying curve at a slightly slower rate.

Early indications from data collected by Professor Strang and his team in a recent study of prisoners[9], which are still under analysis, are of relationships emerging between age and patterns of misuse within prison. This will be of interest in establishing whether such patterns vary from those in the community and is important in helping us understand differences due to imprisonment and further changes that might be made by action by the Service to control and treat drug misuse.

I have illustrated the impact of age on the extent and patterns of misuse. I must also mention that studies have also shown a marked regional variation in misuse of different categories of drug.

Finally, a brief and, possibly, confusing look at some data which have emerged on the extent of misuse within prison.

Table 2

USE IN CUSTODY

CURRENT SENTENCE: Adult Males

%	Drug	n	Study	cp %-community
57	Any	1009	IOP: HIV [7]	77.5 (life)
16	Any	1173	Merseyside [10]	34 (I month)
37	Any	1939	MDT	
57	Cannabis	344	ACMD[1]	70 (life)
32	Cannabis	1939	MDT	
24	Heroin	344	ACMD[1]	31 (life)
03	Opiates	1939	MDT	

The percentage in the left hand column represents the proportion of the prisoners in each study who admitted taking any illicit drug, or the drug specified, during their current sentence.

For purposes of suggesting how much use decreases within prison, the right-hand column of the table provides the percentage of these prisoners who had used in the community, taken from the same study, wherever this was available. One population for whom it is, of course, not available, is the population randomly selected for testing under the Prison Service's mandatory testing programme (shown in the table as MDT) . These MDT results are from the first phase only, representing data from eight establishments gathered over the period February 1995 to August 1995. The extension to all prisons from August 1995 to March 1996 has produced a large body of data, but there is considerable complexity in the analysis of these data and they are still under review.

This table shows much less consistency than the previous ones and is best seen as an indicator of the complexity inherent in interpretation of prevalence data. The only immediate conclusion appears to be that considerably fewer prisoners admitted to using drugs during their current sentence than admitted to having used them prior to entering prison. Some of the differences between the results of the different studies are due to differences such as the two major variables previously mentioned, of age and geography. E.g. the ACMD and Merseyside studies are of single adult prisons in different parts of the country and the MDT programme had a high representation of young offenders, with whom opiate use is much less common than in older age groups.

The results of the eight site first phase of the mandatory testing programme, totalled over the six-month period, indicate a cannabis to heroin ratio, for positive tests, of approximately 11 to 1. This may be compared to a 3.4 to 1 cannabis to heroin ratio for the total of the one year pre-entry data examined previously in Figure 2. However this masks a variation according to age, ie 9 to 1 for those under 21, and 3 to 1 for those aged 24 - 29. The MDT ratio for the total results likewise masks large variations which were found between the eight sites.

The following are some of the main observations which are supported by the preceding tables and figures.

- The prison population contains a much higher proportion of people who have misused drugs in the community, in every age group, than the general population.
- There is a marked decay over time in the numbers using drugs prior to entry to prison; in the studies examined this is from over 70% who have used at some time in their life, to 34% who have used in the preceding month.
- However, this "fall-off" rate appears to be much lower than that for the general population, which exhibits a similar but more rapid effect.
- The extent and pattern of drug misuse varies markedly with age.
- Currently available data on in-prison use shows wide variation in estimates both of all drug use and use of particular drugs, reflecting the many variables in the populations and in the different methodologies used in obtaining the data.
- However fewer prisoners use drugs in prison than have used drugs in the community.

This section would not be complete without a mention of a key area of research which has underpinned the development of the services described in the next section, ie research into the nature and outcomes of prison education, treatment and rehabilitation programmes for substance misusers.

In the development of its drugs strategy, the Prison Service sought expert advice worldwide - through reviews of the literature such as that commissioned from Professor Plant (op cit), expert advisers, and visits to programmes in several other countries, including the USA which contributes the bulk of the literature on service evaluation. It also commissioned a process evaluation of the first "residential" therapeutic programme in the prison service - the ADT (now RAPt) programme at HMP Downview (op. cit). Professor Plant's review suggested that effective programmes:

- are based on social learning theory,
- employ authority structures with clear rules, sanctions, anti-criminal modelling and reinforcement of prosocial behaviour,
- train clients in pragmatic personal and social problem solving,
- have a programme staff that utilizes community resources, encourages empathetic relationships between clients and staff which are characterised by openness and trust,
- employ ex-offender and ex-addict counsellors to serve as credible role-models of successful rehabilitation.

These messages are to a large extent borne out by Player and Martin's findings. Additionally, their review of the ADT programme in HMP Downview provided insight into the necessity for the integration of all programmes into the total prison culture through extensive communication, staff participation and leadership, and commitment from top management, plus the need for a range of programmes to meet the range of differing patterns of misuse.

III. ACTION AND ACTIVITY

The Prison Service's strategy, set out in "Drug Use in Prison"[10], is an integral part of the total Government strategy, "Tackling Drugs Together"[11]. Both documents were published in 1995 and both recognise two fundamental requirements for success:

- overall coordination service-wide with support for, and guidance on, what works, what is needed, and where it may be most effectively provided, and
- local commitment and responses which reflect local conditions and local variation in need.

The Prison Service strategy, therefore, set out its overarching concepts, concerns, and goals, and required that every prison and young offender institution (including prisons under private sector management) formulate its own strategy to meet these central aims, by March 31st 1996. This has been done and the local strategies are currently under review.

Figure 4 illustrates the overarching framework of an integrated strategy intended to control supply, reduce demand and limit risk and associated damage.

Figure 4

THE PRISON SERVICE DRUG STRATEGY

- Reducing the level of drug misuse is a strategic priority for the Prison Service.
- The reduction in drug misuse will be achieved through local drug strategies which will focus on three areas.

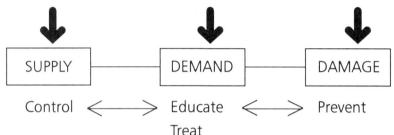

No part stands alone. Reducing demand will lessen supply: diminishing supply will reduce demand, particularly from the experimental and occasional user, and potentially also induce the frequent and dependent user to seek help - especially if there is encouragement and other incentive to do so. Health risks lessen as misuse lessens but awareness, education and other prevention measures - eg hepatitis vaccination and the provision of cleaning agents for injecting equipment - are equally important.

Control has included, to date, the introduction of tighter security measures aimed at uncovering routes of supply, personal possession and use. Measures include random searches of prisoners and their accommodation, use of sniffer dogs on prison sites and increased advice, warnings and support to visitors who may be tempted (or pressured) to smuggle drugs in at visiting times.

As previously mentioned, a programme of mandatory testing of urine samples for illicit drugs was introduced at eight sites in February 1995 and extended to all establishments between August 1995 and March 1996. The programme includes selection of a statistically randomised 10% of inmates in every establishment each month. Positive results incur penalties set by the establishment - commonly days added to the length of sentence. Many establishments have differential schemes for these penalties, characteristically awarding the highest penalty to those who refuse to take the test and the lowest penalty to those testing positive for cannabis.

Both these control measures and the reduction of demand through education and treatment depend upon the identification of drug misusers. Although encouragement of voluntary help-seeking is a cornerstone of the approach, identification by any means should lead to an assessment of need. Such assessments must take into account the characteristics of the user - eg age, gender, sentence length - and the characteristics of misuse, in order for appropriate help to be offered. One prison has set an excellent example of good practice by accompanying notification of a positive test result with a letter advising of the consequences, but also offering referral to help. A letter is also provided to those testing negative so that they can proudly show this to their families on visits.

Help can only be offered if it is available, and a major thrust of the strategy has been the central coordination of a wide range of new services. It was recognised that new programmes needed to be "seeded" geographically, to be introduced to the whole range of establishment types (ie particularly including young offenders and female establishments) and to provide a range of therapeutic techniques. It was also recognised that the development of techniques for local needs analysis would be a key tool in helping to ensure that effective programmes could in future be selected by establishments.

The first phase of the centrally resourced and coordinated programmes started in 1995 and the following table shows where and what type of programmes were developed in 1995/6. It also indicates the provider agencies involved.

Table 3

THERAPEUTIC PROGRAMMES - FIRST WAVE (1995/6)

ESTABLISHMENT	PROGRAMME	PROVIDER
Bristol	Detoxification Unit Relapse Prevention/ Voluntary Testing Unit	In-house
Holme House Channings Wood Portland	Therapeutic Communities (Phoenix House Model)	Tender Tender Tender
Downview	12-Step Rehabilitation	RAPt
Hindley	Educator/Counsellor	Trafford CDT
Holloway	Rehabilitation Unit Detoxification Unit	Cranstoun Tender
Leicester Stocken Ashwell	Needs Analysis	Leicester University
Pentonville	Enhanced 12-Step	RAPt
Swaleside	3-Month Treatment	A.P.A.
Swansea	Detoxification + support	In-house
Wayland	3-Month Treatment	Phoenix House
Yorkshire cluster (8)	Counselling/Community-linked Throughcare	YDRS
All above	Independent Evaluation	PDM Consulting

Twenty two establishments are involved in this first phase, including five young offender institutions and two women's prisons (four others contain some female prisoners). Of the eight establishments in the first wave of mandatory testing, four are also in the first wave of centrally supported therapeutic programmes.

The second phase of introducing new programmes has now started. Bids were made for programmes by interested establishments and thirty establishments were successful. Again there is wide geographical coverage and a wide range of different therapeutic approaches provided by many agencies.

Of particular interest are the two major cluster developments: in Yorkshire in phase 1, and in Kent in phase 2. These recognise that a single establishment cannot provide the full range of therapeutic services to meet all levels of need. Shared provision is needed, with the potential for transferring prisoners to an appropriate programme.

The development has included intensive staff training throughout 1995 and into 1996, from one day general awareness for all staff, to establishment drugs strategy team training, to Diplomas in Addictive Medicine for doctors. In October this year, the Diploma will be available through a long-distance learning scheme and will be open to other categories of staff involved in substance misuse programmes.

This is an overview of the centrally coordinated approach now under way. But only fifty two prisons are involved in the centrally supported introduction of new programmes. What of the others - and is the culture really changing from that described by Professor Gunn in 1989 and quoted earlier?

I have obtained a great deal of insight into changes involving the contribution by health care staff in prisons from this year's annual reports of heads of health care. These reports are required each year from every establishment and, although there is overall freedom to write about local conditions, the Director of Health Care also requests that specific topics be addressed. Provision for drug misuse was one such area for this year's report and the following are excerpts from reports received. They illustrate the good, a good approach experiencing difficulties of resourcing, and evidence that such progress is not universal. I am, however, happy to say that excerpt (c) was very uncharacteristic of the whole.

a)   "The Drug and Alcohol Awareness Committee, chaired by the Senior Medical Officer, meets six times a year. Outside agencies are part of this Committee. The Committee is responsible for the development of the throughcare section of the Drug Strategy Framework Document. Three drug agencies attend the prison and give support to all residential areas. A methadone detoxification programme is available for those inmates who require it. The prison has recently been successful in obtaining funding to operate a Drug Rehabilitation Unit (10 beds) and it is expected to be up and running by September 1996. The unit will concentrate on opiate based dependency. The prison has also introduced to each residential wing its own Drug Liaison officer. These are discipline staff who have been trained to counsel inmates re drug abuse and also liaise with drug agencies as part of throughcare needs. Inmates are also targeted by poster campaigns."

b)   "The programme is for all Mandatory Drug Testing positives, assessed by health care staff and directed to various treatment options - however, this is not happening due to lack of time. The options available, when assessed are:

Drug Awareness Group
Counselling by Health Care Worker
Counselling by Psychologist
Detoxification
District Drugs Advisory Service
Rehabilitation on release"

c)   "Still some drugs are coming in - but not injectables as far as I know. Random urine checks show positive reports. These tests are done periodically since 1995 by discipline staff. We have no serious drug problem and no detoxification facilities."

There is a great deal in the reports to justify optimism and those who have been connected with the Service since the late eighties will, I am sure, agree that the first two excerpts show considerable change on many fronts - not least the evidence of participation and integration of the health care service with multidisciplinary effort.

Finally how will we know if we are doing well?

The single key performance indicator (KPI) chosen for service-wide monitoring to indicate achievement in reducing supply and demand, is as follows:

To ensure that the rate of positive testing for drugs (the number of random drug tests that prove positive) expressed as a percentage of the total number of random drug tests carried out is lower in the fourth quarter of 1996-7 than in the first quarter of that year.

However this is the apex of a pyramid of strategic goals and targets, integrated into the planning process both centrally and at local level.

Secondly as an example of this, is one of the proposed measures for incorporation into the Strategy for Health which is currently the subject of consultation within the Service.

To increase the proportion of inmates year on year testing positive on MDT for Class A drugs, who complete a drug rehabilitation course.

Other essential ways of increasing good practice and high quality provision include investment in training, dissemination of examples of good practice, encouragement of new research and the use of research findings, and publishing official standards.

In this context, the Health Care Standards - published as a subset of the official operating standards for the Prison Service - provide mandatory instructions to governors and health care staff on major areas of health care, with a 3-year term for implementation, following their publication. Health Care Standard 8, "Clinical Services for Substance Misusers", was issued in 1995 and fully meets Professor Gunn's requirement for the "introduction of a standard opiate withdrawal regime" (op cit). Further planned Standards - e.g. on throughcare - will also contribute to the achievement of the aims of the Prison Service's drugs strategy.

IV.   FOR CONSIDERATION AND DISCUSSION

There are three areas where, I believe, development of both theory and practical techniques are of importance to the success of the Service's strategy. The areas are:

- availability/accessibility
- targeting, prevention and treatment
- measuring success or failure

The need for widespread provision is suggested by the knowledge that the Service is facing major growth in its population, as well as a major expansion in the numbers misusing drugs in the community. Recent findings on drug use among the young - some of which have been presented to you - describe continuing increase. John Balding concludes from his five year study of schoolchildren [12] :"the percentage of boys and of girls aged 12-13 years recording illicit drug use in 1995 is greater than the figures for 15-16 year olds in 1987". There has been a very large increase in use of illicit drugs by schoolchildren between 1987 and 1995.

If this does not change, then a relatively rapid growth in the demand for effective services in prisons must be predicted. More than ever, we will have to ensure the best possible use of resources through demonstrably effective programmes, with targeting of areas with the potential for greatest gain.

The thought that we will be facing, an ever increasing problem, with a corresponding need for increased success in dealing with it, introduces the following diagram.

Figure 5

PREVENTION TARGETING

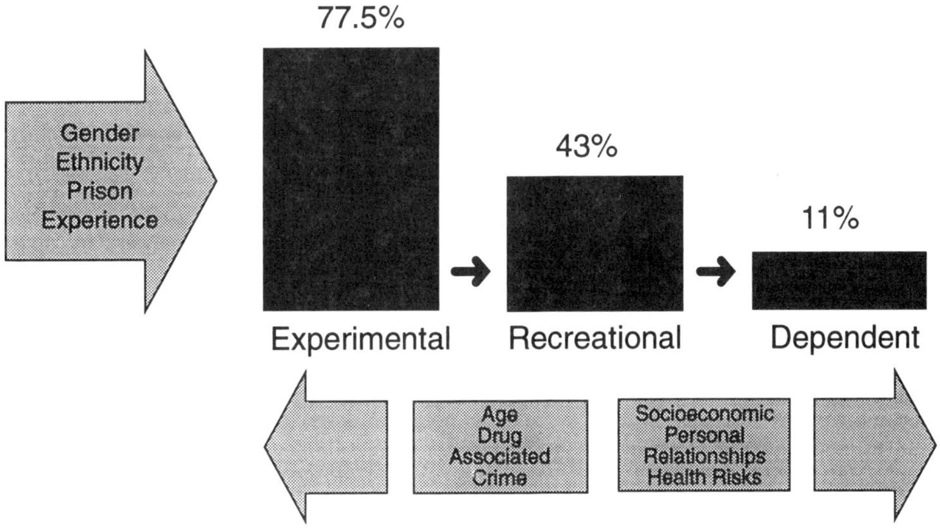

The boxes in the diagram represent the commonly agreed "progression" and decay in numbers which characterise types of drug using behaviour. Their size has been estimated from the results of the studies examined earlier. If the number of experimental users increases, it is likely that the size of the populations represented by the other boxes will also do so. This may not be a proportional effect, as this shift to dependency is undoubtedly affected by many other variables which could alter.

However progression is associated with increasing damage to the individual and to society. The weight of numbers on the left is counterweighted by the severity of this damage on the right. Successfully educating and treating those in each category will mean targeting and severing the "links". We need good understanding of the cultural and individual causes of progression from stage to stage, in the community and in prison, in order to provide appropriate education and practical support.

The diagram lists some of the known factors which vary along with the progression between the three categories. The diagram also lists some "conditioners" - ie factors which influence the patterns of misuse, and possibly dimensions, in each category including experience in prison. The intention is to provoke discussion on elements that are missing, on the relative importance of these factors and how knowledge of these and their inter-relationships can contribute to the development of effective services.

Understanding the complexity of the relationships portrayed in the last diagram is important not only for the effective development and targeting of services, but also for the valid interpretation of data collected on provision and outcomes.

Table 2 showed that generalised conclusions cannot be drawn from data from a single source - whether a single establishment or a single methodology. The misuse of drugs has many aetiological factors and many inter-related and confounding variables, some of which have already been mentioned. The ACMD report (op cit) has recognised this in its suggestion of a "performance profile" for the measurement of service provided by prisons and its outcome. Twenty items are proposed which fall into four broad categories:

- prevalence indices,
- amount of service provision and utilisation,
- indices of impact and outcomes,
- indices of quality of services provided.

V. CONCLUSION

In conclusion I offer a personal statement of faith based, as I explained at the start, on cautious, but informed, optimism. I believe that this is an era of major opportunity for the Prison Service to effect change which will benefit its prisoners, its staff, and society, and that major efforts in this direction are already underway.

The Prison Service is not responsible for the escalation of illicit drug use in society, nor can it eradicate it. However, it has a major contribution to make: for individuals, in reducing the health risks and chaos that such misuse can bring to their lives, and for society, which bears the consequences of that chaos and risk.

The Service has made substantial and rapid progress towards making that contribution. We need to secure, increase and improve on that progress. We need to determine what works best and, when this is determined, we have a moral obligation to do it as best we can.

REFERENCES

1. Report by the Advisory Council on the Misuse of Drugs Part III: Drug Misusers and the Prison System - An Integrated Approach. HMSO 1996. ISBN 0 11 341158 8
2. Gunn J, Maden T, Swinton M. Mentally Disordered Prisoners. Home Office may 1991 (Rev). ISBN 0 86252 689 2
3. Plant M. The Management of Problem Drug Use in Prisons: A Review. Report to the Research & Planning Unit, Home Office. University of Edinburgh 1995
4. Player E, Martin C. A Preliminary Evaluation of the ADT Treatment Programme at HMP Downview. Report to the Home Office October 1995
5. The Task Force to Review Services for Drug Misusers. Report of an Independent Review of Drug Treatment Services in England. Department of Health April 1996. H87/001/04/96/0032
6. Mott J, Mirrlees-Black C. Self-Reported Drug Misuse in England & Wales: Findings from the 1992 British Crime Survey. Home Office Research & Planning Unit Paper 89 1995. ISBN 1 85893 351 X
7. Meltzer H, Gill B, Petticrew M, Hinds K. The Prevalence of Psychiatric Morbidity Among Adults Living in Private Households. OPCS 1995. ISBN 0 11 691627 3
8. Bridgwood A, Malbon G. Survey of the Physical Health of Prisoners. OPCS 1995. ISBN 0 11 691639 7
9. Strang J, et al. HIV/AIDS : Knowledge, Attitudes and Behaviour of Adult Male Prisoners in England & Wales. Unpublished report to the Home Office Research & Planning Unit Nov 1995.
10. HM Prison Service. Drug Misuse In Prison. Strategy Document for the Prison Service, England & Wales. Directorate of Health Care HMPS 1995.
11. HM Government. Tackling Drugs Together: A Strategy for England 1995-1998. HMSO May 1995. ISBN 0 10 128462 4
12. Balding J. Young People and Illegal Drugs in 1996. Schools Health Education Unit, University of Exeter 1996. ISBN 0 85068 174X

TACKLING THE PROBLEM

Robin Pitt, Drug Strategy Team, HM Prison Service

Several years before the Government White Paper "Tackling Drugs Together" was published, HMP Long Lartin's Corporate Management Group (CMG) recognised that a drug problem existed at the prison and began to set objectives to address these issues. These objectives were closely mirrored by the Prison Service document "Drug Misuse in Prisons" which followed the White Paper. Long Lartin's list of objectives included:

* understanding the dynamics of drug dealing and distribution within the establishment
* discovering the quantity and purity of drugs entering the prison
* introduction of measures to combat the importation of drugs (reducing supply)
* reducing the demand for drugs

The CMG also recognised the need for a separate committee to co-ordinate the drug related initiatives, the membership being drawn from all the prison's specialisms. By 1994 a number of initiatives were in place which included:

Reducing demand

* **Education** - information was circulated to all staff and inmates regarding substance misuse to raise awareness of the potential dangers involved
* **Drug Liaison Officers** - these were basic grade officers who received two day Drug Awareness Courses delivered by the Psychology and Health Care Departments. The officers' task was to identify misusers and encourage them to participate in the psychological interventions available and the detoxification programme if required. The aim was to have a Drug Liaison Officer (DLO) on each of the prison wings
* **Psychological interventions** - were in two formats; a Holding Group was run where misusers could meet on a weekly basis and from which they might be motivated towards detoxification or other 'therapy'; an Action Group was run for those who had completed detoxification and who sought to maintain a drug free state by way of group therapy.
* **Physiological detoxification** - (for opiate misuse) was either by way of an in-patient Di-hydrocodeine based reduction programme or Lofexedine programme for those who did not wish admission to the Health Care Centre.
* **Drug Free Wing** (Voluntary Testing Unit) - this facility was opened some two years ago. 70% of its population was drawn from those who abstained from drugs on moral or religious grounds and the remaining 30% from those who sought to achieve a drug free state.
* **One-to-One Counselling** - was made available from a limited number of appropriately trained and skilled staff. They were originally located within Psychology, Health Care and Probation.
* **Rehabilitation Unit** - this unit is due to open shortly and is funded from the second tranche of bids made to the DHC last September. It will consist of a trial unit of 8 beds designed to accommodate misusers for periods of up to 4 months with the emphasis upon long term behavioural change. If successful the unit will be extended to 30 beds and accept misusers from the whole of the Dispersal Estate.

Combating the importation of drugs

* **Searching** - with limited staffing available the opportunity to make a real impact was limited. However, an understanding of the dynamics of dealing and distribution also produced greatly improved intelligence gathering resulting in information leading to a number of quite spectacular results. Following the publication of the Woodcock and Learmont reports and the availability of a dedicated search team, even greater impact has been made in this area.

Breaking the chain

Another tactic employed was to cause chaos in the cartels by identifying dealers and runners and shipping them out at the earliest opportunity. Whilst others would soon take their place, this served to break the chain and keep the organisation off balance. The success of these operations was measured by way of false alarm bells, a traditional way in the Dispersal Estate of expressing dissatisfaction. If dealers are 'shipped out', there will be no false alarm bells - everyone will be delighted to see their debts go with them!

Quantity and Purity
As a result of the statistics quoted in the Dynamics of Dealing and Distribution, seizures were occasionally submitted for a quantitative analysis to the local forensic science laboratory. This procedure offering an opportunity of measuring the weight and purity as well as ascertaining common adulterants used. This enabled the Medical Officers to measure the extent of a habit and to prescribe appropriate treatments during detoxification. In consequence it has never been considered necessary to prescribe Methadone.

Measuring performance of the detoxification initiative
Apart from knowing the number of successful detoxifications (proven by regular urine testing using ONTRACK imuno-assay prior to MDT) it was also possible to calculate the financial impact upon dealers by the following method: Number of inmates undergoing detoxification multiplied by the number of bags of heroin they would normally have consumed during that detoxification period.

Thus even if the detoxification is unsuccessful, if the inmate has not taken heroin during the attempt then the dealers suffer a financial loss. Publication of such figures can prove a significant incentive to staff who might otherwise consider detoxification a waste of valuable resources. Measuring performance in this manner demonstrates a loss to the dealers of around £80,000 per annum.

The dynamics of dealing and distribution
There were a number of misusers seeking to maintain their habit by coercing partners/friends to bring in small quantities of drugs through visits. Such importations were poorly planned and often ill conceived attempts resulting in occasional finds by searchers. Nevertheless, a significant quantity of drugs entered the prison as a result. This was probably of as much concern to the established dealers as it was to Security, serving as it undoubtedly did to reduce the dealers' potential profit margins. Of far greater concern were the professionally organised importations of quantities of drugs destined to be marketed by the dealers to addicted inmates throughout the establishment. Such deliveries would often be received by more than one inmate at visits, initially being concealed within the vagina/anus of the visitor, wrapped in cling film, and smeared with Vaseline prior to insertion. These techniques together with strong body odour from the orifices serving to mask the smell of the drug made detection by dogs unlikely.

Once in prison, the drugs would be delivered to the dealer by the carriers, the dealer then adulterating the substance to maximise profits before dividing into the appropriate number of bags or folds.

In the case of heroin, a £70 gram purchased from outside (with an average street purity of around 25%) would be further adulterated and divided into 20 bags each retailing at £10. Runners would then deliver the bags to the users, their payment being a free bag for every four delivered.

Credit would be extended to those with proven wealth in which event they would be supplied with a bank account number for family or friends to pay into thus minimising risks of detection. Those without credit status would be required to smuggle money into the prison to pay their debts or to pay by way of tobacco/phone cards. Some desperate users would resort to sexual favours to pay off their creditors. In at least one instance, an inmate admitted to satisfying his appetite for young men by watching out for those threatened as a result of non payment of debts.

The dealers required a complex organisational network in order to operate. In addition to carriers and runners, they required 'holders' who would normally be inmates trusted by staff and upon whom suspicion was least likely to fall. Heavies were employed to make sure that the market was protected. They also needed links with dealers outside of prison and sometimes go-betweens both inside and outside of the establishment. It was quite common for receptions to be given a free bag or two in order to establish a bond and create an addiction. Debtors refusing or unable to pay were the subject of a contract - 4 or 5 bags being offered to any user to mark or seriously injure the offender.

Perhaps the greatest surprise in store for CMG was to discover that there were around 70 users of heroin in the prison at any one time consuming an average of 1.5 bags daily. This meant that the value of that particular drugs market alone amounted to £1,050 per day, £31,500 per month, £378,000 per annum.

THE MANAGEMENT OF SUBSTANCE ABUSE IN PRISON
THE HMP WANDSWORTH MODEL

Bill Thurbin, Throughcare Co-ordinator
& Dave Savage, Prison Officer

The purpose of our presentation is to show how our prison's Substance Misuse Management Strategy is developing, one year on from the issuing of the Government's White Paper, *'Tackling Drugs Together'*.

HMP Wandsworth formulated its local strategy from the Prison Service's own Policy and Strategy Statements. The Prison's Strategy Group was first formed with the circulation of the Government's Green Paper in 1994. The group consisted of people of many different disciplines from throughout the prison including representatives from probation, healthcare, psychology, security, induction, Board of Visitors and discipline staff.

Meeting so early during the White Paper's evolution, together with the willingness and co-operation of key players in the prison, helped in the completion of HMP Wandsworth's comprehensive strategy. Having a needs analysis completed by our Psychology Department in the early days of the Group enabled us to identify where resources should ideally be channelled. Once completed, the Strategy formed the backbone of our bid to the Prison Service Healthcare Directorate, asking for money to fund the project. I am pleased to say that we will receive funding for the next three years.

We also saw the necessity of integrating our efforts with agency services in the wider community thus providing greater throughcare opportunities for inmates in our charge. Having representations on the local DAT, DRG and the SLDPT will ensure that the prison is considered in any wider strategies that are being implemented in our area.

Let us now look at some of the key elements of the strategy.

Mandatory Drug Testing: Talking Points

- A Mandatory Drug Testing Programme (MDT) for prisoners was introduced in Wandsworth in February 1996. We were among the last of the establishments to introduce the programme so our experience is to some extent limited.

- The programme requires prisoners to provide a urine sample for testing purposes and it is now a disciplinary offence within Wandsworth (and indeed all other prisons) for a prisoner to use a controlled drug without appropriate medical authorisation.

- Whilst we are not qualified to draw conclusions about the efficiency of MDT as a policy nationally, we are qualified to talk about MDT in Wandsworth. Locally we have found little evidence of a shift to harder drugs and in fact we feel that far from diverting attention and resources away from treatment programmes, MDT has become an invaluable strand in Wandsworth's substance misuse management strategy.

- Let us firstly look at how MDT assists at reducing the demand for controlled drugs in the establishment.
  - * Clearly the Mandatory Drug Testing Programme (even months after its introduction) is a common talking point between prisoners. Mandatory Drug Testing has an undeniable deterrent effect. Since the introduction of testing, there has been much anecdotal evidence of prisoners refraining from drug use. It is too new a policy in Wandsworth to gain any reliable statistical evidence.
  - * Obviously, some prisoners (incidentally, quite a small proportion at Wandsworth) have continued to misuse drugs and many of them have been identified through Mandatory Drug Testing. However, this identification of prisoners still misusing is in itself positive. All prisoners testing positive are referred to Wing Drug Liaison Officers who will attempt treatment options, both in Wandsworth and in other prisons. We have found that some prisoners are actually pleased that their drug misuse has been detected and that someone has offered them help.
  - * For prisoners identified as persistent drug misusers, MDT has also given us the power, with the Frequent Testing Programme, to place the prisoner on a programme of regular tests. We are concerned at Wandsworth that this should never become a punitive programme but should instead be accompanied by treatment, advice and counselling. In these circumstances the

Frequent Testing Programme will become a positive incentive helping the prisoner to avoid relapsing back into misuse.

* Thinking more globally, the Mandatory Drug Testing Programme and the statistics it produces have allowed us to build a responsive strategy.

With the results of MDT tests over the last few months, we have been able to construct a fairly reliable picture of the scale and extent of drug misuse within the prison. We have been able to gain an indication of:

• which drugs are most commonly misused within the prison.

• the extent to which these drugs are being misused.

• in which locations, by which particular group of prisoners, these drugs are being misused.

So far from diverting resources from treatment and rehabilitation, MDT has allowed us to target those resources more effectively. We can now ask:

• are our treatment programmes appropriate for the groups of prisoners misusing illicit drugs? Does our strategy offer enough short-term treatment for drug-misusing remand prisoners (who MDT has consistently identified as being more likely to misuse drugs whilst in the prison)?

• are the programmes we offer consistent with the types of drug regularly being misused?

Instead of aiming resources blindly, MDT has given us the ability to use our resources cost-effectively to tackle those drugs and prisoners identified. We believe MDT at Wandsworth has a role in reducing the demand for drugs in this way. Of course if we are correct in this assumption, the Mandatory Drug Testing Programme will also assist in reducing the supply of drugs into the establishment. We have already received much intelligence suggesting that the market for drugs in Wandsworth is not as buoyant as it once was. We have heard of suppliers unable to sell and being forced to hold large amounts of illicit drugs. Of course this in itself means that those prisoners are far more likely to be identified as suppliers through the normal routine of searching and intelligence gathering. We have also seen prisoners who believe MDT represents a positive response to drug problems at Wandsworth, and they have been a little more willing to offer information about suppliers and methods of supply.

The Throughcare Process
Any prisoner who enters the prison, has to undergo a brief medical screening, regardless of whether he is a newly sentenced prisoner or if he has been in the system for a while. During the screening a doctor will ask a series of questions to ascertain the health of the prisoner and to discover whether there are any problems that should be brought to the medical staff's attentions. Some of the questions relate to the inmate's drug/alcohol use. From there the inmate may go to the Primary Detox Facility.

Primary Detox Facility
If it becomes apparent that the inmate has a problem with his substance misuse, he will be offered primary chemical detox. When HMP Wandsworth's hospital is refurbished at the end of this year, it will be equipped with a fifteen bed designated detox ward with three nurses trained in this area of work. The period that the chemical detox will last is between 7-10 days (for opiates). An inmate may detox for longer with other substances (such as benzodiazepines) depending on the severity of the user's addiction. Towards the end of the detox period a nurse will complete a detox summary, giving details of how the inmate has managed during the detox and if he is motivated to continue with some other form of therapy/treatment to address his substance misuse. With the agreement of the inmate, this summary will be forwarded to either the post detox support area (based on K1 landing) or the Substance Misuse Throughcare Co-ordinator.

This summary will serve as an introduction. If the inmate is not happy to access these services, then he will be returned to normal location with details on how to access these services at a later date if he changes his mind.

The inmate may choose to go to The Post Detox Support Area. This landing, currently being used as a temporary hospital during the mentioned refurbishment, will provide a 24 bed detox support area for those inmates completing primary chemical detox when the landing is freed from its temporary purpose at the end of this year.

Negotiations are under way with the Rehabilitation of Addicted Prisoners Trust (RAPt) to provide a treatment programme based on the 12 steps disease/medical model. Specially trained prison officers will be used to support the programme and to get involved in this therapeutic regime. Inmates would be expected in accordance with the requirements of the 12 steps model to remain abstinent during this post detox period. To ensure that abstinence is maintained, inmates will go on a voluntary urine testing programme. This may be continued by the inmate, if he has found this helpful, once he has left the post detox area. At the end of this period, the inmate will be referred to the Substance Misuse Throughcare Co-ordinator (with the inmate's permission) to discuss how he would like to continue his therapy/treatment for the rest of his sentence.

The Substance Misuse Throughcare Co-ordinator (SMTCO)
Inmates can be referred to the SMTCO from various sources throughout the prison. These include:
- Self referral
- Primary detox facility
- Post detox area
- Probation/chaplaincy/psychology depts
- Personal officers
- Family/friends via the Prison Visitors Centre as well as Mandatory Drug Testing

It is important to say that all positive result inmates will be visited by the SMTCO or his representatives and made aware of the treatment services available and how to access them.

The role of the SMTCO is to:

- Facilitate the access of external service providers to the prison
- Provide training/briefings to prison staff on substance misuse; helping substance misusers; accessing service providers; the overall prison strategy and the local strategy
- Co-ordinate the Assessment and Referral package
- Co-ordinate the provision of groupwork programmes within the prison which are cognitive behavioural in their essence
- Manage staff chosen as Wing Liaison Officers (WLO) - this post is unique in the Prison Service

The Wing Liaison Officer Scheme (WLO)
Inmates who have been referred to the SMTCO by the sources mentioned earlier will be logged for monitoring purposes. The SMTCO will then pass the relevant details of the referred inmate on to the Wing Liaison Officer (WLO). The WLOs are based on each wing and will approach the inmate and explain that he has been referred and ask if he wants to start/continue treatment/therapy. All inmates will be given information about the WLO scheme and advice on harm reduction during the three-day induction programme when they enter the prison.

If the inmate says that he is not interested, he will be left information on how he can access service provision if he changes his mind later on in his sentence. If the inmate says that he is interested, he will be invited by the WLO to fill in an assessment and referral plan. This assessment and referral plan seeks to:
- Identify the inmate's strengths and weaknesses in past attempts to address his substance misuse.
- Identify areas in the inmate's life that may cause high risk situations, opening an avenue for some brief intervention work.
- Help the inmate identify the connection between his substance misuse and criminal activity (if there is one).
- Find out whether the inmate wants to access: medical treatment because of his substance misuse (detox); a blood test to identify sero-prevalent infections (with the opportunity to have pre and post test counselling); the proposed Hepatitis B inoculation programme due to start later this year.
- Help the inmate look at where he wants to be with his substance misuse in 1 month, 3

months, 6 months and 1 year's time.
- Identify whether the inmate wants his family involved and kept up to date with his progress.
- Refer the inmate to internal/external service providers, depending on the goals set by the inmate.

Using the suggestions the inmate has made regarding what he wants to do with his drug/alcohol use, the WLO and inmate draw up an action plan together, a therapeutic contract between the prison and the user. The WLO will then encourage, support and guide the inmate to achieve the goals that he has set for himself. Some of the goals that have been set may prove impractical for the inmate to achieve by himself because of his incarceration. The WLO will automatically visit the inmate at 1 month, 3 months and 6 months (longer if necessary) to see if the inmate is achieving the goals he has set for himself and to evaluate or change those goals if they prove impractical. Any goals set will be incorporated into the inmate's sentence plan. Particular attention will be given to those inmates approaching the end of their sentence, encouraging links to external service providers to ensure the throughcare process continues beyond the prison gate.

Services
Proposed services that inmates will be able to access or be referred on to include:
- Detox
- Post detox therapy/treatment
- A cognitive behavioural programme run by Prison Officers
- Prisoners Resource Service Remand Team, Criminal Justice Worker
- Prisoners Resource Service Convicted Team, drug/alcohol worker (upon request)
- Narcotics Anonymous group session
- Alcoholics Anonymous group session
- The Wing Liaison Officer Scheme
- Acupuncture during the detox and post detox stage
- Access to external service providers from the area to which the inmate wants to return upon release
- Transfer to another prison offering a therapeutic regime that would be more conducive to the inmate's needs
- Community Care Assessment.

The Role of Security in Substance Misuse Strategy
The Substance Misuse Strategy at HMP Wandsworth is reinforced by the high profile security measures in place at the prison. It would be inappropriate to disclose the details of these measures except to say that they are constantly reviewed and improved in line with current requirements of the Home Office.

In reducing the availability of illicit and illegal substances through search procedures and intelligence gathering, the security department provides a positive support and contribution to the quality of life for inmates and staff within the prison. Friends and family who may have been subject to pressures to supply the substances misused, also benefit from the procedures, they are aware of the greater chances of being detected in possession and are able to use this as justification not to supply.

The intelligence gathered by the security department provides a wide variety of information, from the types and quantity of substance being brought into the establishment to the inmates to be targeted for Mandatory Drug Testing under reasonable suspicion.

One of the most effective tools in addressing substance misuse in the prison environment is information. At HMP Wandsworth a high value is placed on delivering good quality, current information in useful form for inmates and staff. To this end, staff receive training sessions in substance misuse awareness, supported by updated information provided by the Substance Misuse Throughcare Co-ordinator through Wing Liaison Officers at wing meetings and on demand.

When inmates are received at the prison, they take part in an induction programme designed to prepare them for their time in custody. To ensure that they are aware of the services available, and the regulations and practices governing the running of prison life. An integral part of the course is a session on substance misuse, staff of the Induction Unit present a specifically designed package, giving general information on the possible hazards or effects of substance misuse, with an explanation of Mandatory

Drug Testing in prisons, and the prison rules governing misuse.

Great emphasis is placed on providing the details of services available for inmates requiring help in addressing substance misuse and the methods of access, the session is supported by a printed handout that inmates can retain for future reference.

For inmates approaching release, there are development courses available, designed to improve communication and information gathering skills; they include sessions on substance misuse. The sessions involve coping strategies for alcohol misuse, explored through the medium of role play and discussion groups. Building on the abilities of the group and individuals to recognise the factors leading to misuse, this is linked to the offending cycle and how misuse affects others as well as the misuser. In conjunction with the Substance Misuse Throughcare Co-ordinator, the sessions are being reviewed and redeveloped, to provide access to a greater number of inmates through drop-in courses and Substance Misuse specific programmes made available to everyone.

HMP Wandsworth's Substance Misuse Strategy is still in its infancy and has a long way to go until it reaches maturity. It would be easy to dwell on the Prison Service's past inadequacies in its approach to caring for inmates with substance misuse problems. At last things appear to be changing for the better. The publication of the Government's White Paper and the Prison Service's response 'Drug Misuse in Prison', have given HMP Wandsworth's Drug Strategy Team a clear and cohesive direction. We look forward to the future where Throughcare for Substance Misusers in Prison *means* Throughcare for Substance Misusers in Prison.

The recent Department of Health Task Force to Review Services for Drug Misusers stated that:

'Better use should be made of opportunities presented by the Criminal Justice System. In particular, the Prison Service should take account of our recommendation relating to treatments and ensure consistency and continuity of care for those entering prison, during their sentence and on release.'

With our Strategy in place, we aim to achieve just that.

THE PRISON SERVICE DRUG STRATEGY - AN OUTSIDER'S VIEW

Mike Trace, Director, RAPt and
Paddy Costall, Head of Criminal Justice, Cranstoun Projects

Mike Trace introduced the seminar. While this was an outsider's view, at the moment it was complimentary to the Prison Service. Areas for discussion were along the lines of debate between professionals rather than criticism of a statutory authority. He said the presenters would not waste much time on giving information on how the strategy was created, as this was dealt with elsewhere. He did, however, want to make a couple of preliminary points before going on to the two main areas of the strategy: Mandatory Drug Testing and Treatment Service Provision.

The first preliminary point was on the issue of key performance indicators. The fact that the only key performance indicator on the drug strategy was the number of positive urine tests under MDT could be misleading - measures of success of a drug strategy should be much broader, encompassing measurement of the level of drug related misbehaviour in the prison, the smooth functioning of the regime and the provision of diversion and treatment services to inmates. The audience's attention was drawn to the ACMD report on Drug Misuse in Prison and, in particular, to the draft list of performance indicators included in that document which could be used by prison managers as a much more comprehensive measurement of the effectiveness of any individual establishment's drug strategy. Concentrating solely on the KPI of Mandatory Drug Tests was too simplistic.

The second preliminary point related to the funding of treatment initiatives in prison. While welcoming the Prison Service's recent investment in treatment, the relatively small scale of Prison Service resources available for this purpose was highlighted, when compared to the amount spent on drug misuse by the Department of Health and Community Care Authorities. There was a current concern that as the Prison Service started to put money into services, the Health Authorities and Local Authorities would take money out on a much larger scale. This issue was being addressed by the Central Drugs Co-ordination Unit who were trying to agree a national framework for purchasing services in prison and aftercare services for people leaving prison. The presenters hoped that the resulting advice to DATs would encourage more consistent purchasing at a local level. Audience members were encouraged to take part in this process.

Mike then went on to make a short presentation on Mandatory Drug Testing. After a brief history of how it had been implemented and progress so far, he proceeded to raise the following issues:

1. **What were the objectives of the MDT programme?**
   It was primarily an information gathering measure, and a deterrent to prisoners considering using drugs in prison.
2. **The organisation of the system**.
   Contrary to some people's predictions, the implementation of the programme had been well organised and avoided procedural pitfalls.
3. **The figures so far.**
   The overall positive rate had gone down nationally from an average rate of 36% during the pilot period, Feb-June 1995, to under 30% in the last three months. However, there seemed to be an increase in the number of positives for opiates during the same period. The audience was urged to take these figures with caution, as fluctuating results could be an indicator of what was happening in the prison, but could also be an indicator of the purity of the testing process and the ability of prisoners to get round it.
4. **The problems associated with MDT**
   Possible problems could be the over emphasis of resources and time on one single element of the strategy, the process of prisoners transferring from cannabis to Class A drugs and the inappropriate targeting of casual cannabis users.
5. **The options for the future**.
   a) Carry on as the programme is now
   b) Carry on the MDT programme but vary the penalties that are being made as a result of positive tests.

c) Carry on the testing programme but cease testing for cannabis
d) Scrap the MDT programme and invest the money in drug using surveys and a higher level of investment in treatment.

This section of the presentation was of great interest to the audience and there was a long period of questioning. Issues raised were :

- that it was unfair to extrapolate too much from the early figures from MDT as throughout this year new prisons had come on stream which would skew the figures.
- that it was in fact fair to target cannabis as this was the main cause of bullying and intimidation in prisons.
- that it would be wrong for the Prison Service to take any other line than zero tolerance for any drug use within a prison.
- that if the prioritising of resources was the issue than surely it was better to spend resources on people with serious drug problems.
- that the amount of extra days awarded for a positive drug test resulted in a drain on resources for the Prison Service at a time when overcrowding was a problem.
- that the deterrent effect of MDT was starting to take effect.
- that the amount of time it takes to get a test analysed was starting to become a problem, particularly in those prisons where treatment programmes relied on urine testing.
- that there was little evidence to show that people were transferring from cannabis to other drugs.
- that self report surveys were a useful alternative as a way of gathering information on the level of drug use in a prison.
- that MDT was not primarily a security tool but an encouragement into treatment.

———————— ● ————————

Paddy Costall focused on the role treatment services were perceived to play and how this vision had been achieved. His aim was to stimulate discussion, not to provide a definitive critique. It was particularly important to state at the beginning that he believed issues related to drug use affected all those in the prison environment and not just those engaged in the delivery, or receipt, of treatment.

The Strategy
Based on figures in the recently published ACMD report *(Drug Misusers and the Prison System - An Integrated Approach)* there were in the region of 5,000 drug-dependent individuals in the prison system at any one time. Some estimates put the figures much higher. The strategy made a clear statement about the diversity of treatment required within the system, addressing the needs of all prisoners. Local needs assessments should guide individual establishments in developing relevant services, which ranged from education and self-help, through advice and counselling, to designated treatment units. It is obvious that all needs identified could not practically be met in every one of the 133 prison establishments. However reference was made to using transfers to facilitate a prisoner's entry to appropriate treatment, where necessary.

Examples of this could be seen in the arrangements for clusters of prisons in Yorkshire and in Kent. The roles of the various agencies which might be involved were briefly mentioned, including the importance of after-care arrangements. There was also a general statement about governors making provision in their financial plans for purchasing services. This, however, made no reference to the availability of resources centrally, which was particularly important in the light of the 13.3% cut in expenditure imposed on the Prison Service over the next 3 years.

The Response
As has been said, much enthusiasm was generated by the strategy, with most prisons looking upon it as an important tool in tackling the problems associated with illicit drug use. Agencies outside the Prison Service broadly welcomed it as the first open acknowledgment of the scale of the problem; also it provided some positive ideas for how to deal with it. Initially the impetus was behind the security measures,

particularly MDT. This was largely media driven, through strident headlines, with ministers responding to public concern that "something must be done immediately".

However the experience of his own agency, working in over 40 establishments in the South-East, had been that operational staff within the prisons had taken a more balanced view. They saw the inadvisability of a single-track approach to tackling drugs in their establishments. *Interestingly, in Scotland the implementation of MDT was delayed while the prisons developed services to offer alternatives to those who wished to avail themselves of them.*

A lot of time and energy in the Directorate of Healthcare was devoted to the establishment of a series of pilot programmes, funded centrally, across a number of establishments and employing a variety of treatment methods. The first phase of these, 13 in all, were almost all in place. Contracts for running them were put out to competitive tender and they were all to be independently evaluated to determine their effectiveness.

These programmes were to be welcomed, particularly as attempts to create genuine partnerships with the Prison Service. However they could also be described as "scratching the surface", in terms of the overall response to the problem. There was a need to address the problem of drug use in prison in the wider context. The commitment of significant resources to a number of high profile programmes, to the exclusion of other forms of intervention, may be a mistake. An overall approach required a number of components to deliver quality and effective services, which would be accessed by greater numbers of prisoners. The cost of the pilots was in the region of £2m. The programmes may provide services for around 1500 prisoners in a year. The Prisoner's Resource Service, in the past 2 years, provided services to over 1100 prisoners each year. The comparative cost was £450,000 per year. He was not seeking to make a plea for resources for PRS, but to illustrate the point about resource allocation generally.

The recent Task Force Review of drug services in England noted that the criminal justice system generally presents an important opportunity for identifying drug users and encouraging them into treatment. They also noted the need for improvement in this area. This concern extended to the range and accessibility of services available to prisons and continuity of provision on release. Related to the latter point, and integral to the joint working of agencies in the prison setting, is the issue of community care assessments. A recent survey, published by SCODA, found serious problems for prisoners in accessing assessments. Locally some of this may be overcome by negotiation, but guidance issued centrally may provide more impetus to the process.

Resources

The question of who was responsible for funding for drugs services in prisons was answered in different ways, depending on the respondent. Obviously the Prison Service was making a significant commitment, via the treatment programmes being piloted by the Directorate of Health Care. But these may be only scratching the surface of the problem. Health Authorities have, up until now, played a major role in funding services. The Probation Service, via partnership monies, have also contributed. With pressure increasing on rapidly diminishing resources, there was a lack of clarity on where future funding should come from.

This lack of clarity, or responsibility, could seriously impede the implementation of the strategy and serve to undermine the enthusiasm and confidence of those charged with its implementation. Recent meetings involving the Prison Service, Home Office, Department of Health, Probation Services, Health Authorities and independent providers of drug services, convened by the Central Drug Co-ordination Unit, had begun to identify the areas where work needed to be done. There was an obvious role for Drug Action Teams in the process. It was vital that the Prison Service was represented in the DAT structure and that this representation was used effectively to bring prison drug services into the mainstream of provision. Failure to recognise the key role these services play will have consequences not only for prisoners and prisons, but for society generally. To miss the opportunity to engage drug users in services, at a time of obvious crisis, would indeed be false economy in the longer-term.

Harm reduction and prescribing

Health Care Standard 8, which was concerned with clinical standards for substance misusers, was issued at the same time as the strategy. It sought to ensure that the services available to prisoners were compatible with those in the wider community. The strategy made specific reference to the prescribing of methadone to prisoners. Whilst stating abstinence as the ultimate goal, the strategy, and the Standard, stated clearly that methadone prescribing should be an option available in all prisons. The obvious beneficiaries of such a policy were those on remand and serving short sentences, who had been on maintenance regimes prior to admission.

There was also recognition of the value of methadone as part of a detoxification programme for prisoners who request this. The strategy made clear that prisoners on such programmes and regimes were still subject to MDT, in relation to unprescribed medication, with all the associated sanctions. Paddy was unaware of any research into the extent to which Health Care Standard 8 was being implemented. Feedback he had from his own teams suggested that prescribing practices were largely determined by the attitude of the Senior Medical Officer of the individual prisons. Concerns existed around continuity of care for those prisoners subject to transfer around the system.

Response from prison drug services

From December 1994 a network of British Prison Drug Services had been meeting, with a view to developing standards of practice within prisons. There had been 3 seminars, the last, in Glasgow, in March, attracting over 90 participants, from all disciplines, including prison staff. Copies of the standards produced have been distributed widely and the network continues to grow. The Network was the British arm of a wider European Network, coordinated by PRS, with funding from the EU, which aims to disseminate good practice throughout the 15 member states and beyond.

PRISONERS' FAMILIES - SCAPEGOATS OR PARTNERS IN CRIME?
Lucy Gampell (Co-ordinator, Federation of Prisoners' Families Support Groups) & Joanna Morgan (Training & Development Officer, ADFAM National)

Lucy Gampell explained that the presentation would be based around the experiences of families as reported to the Federation and on the training for Visitors' Centre staff FPFSG had been doing with ADFAM National.

The perception of families, and organisations working with them, was that there appeared to be an assumption made by the Prison Service that families were the main culprits as regards bringing drugs into prison. Participants were asked to suggest routes by which drugs came into prison in order to highlight that these are *multifarious* and that prisoners' families, whilst undoubtedly responsible for some of the illicit material, were by no means the only source. These included: social visits; official visits; prison staff (officers, chaplaincy, education etc); over the wall; receptions; day release; and release on temporary licence. It was important to bear this in mind, and to be aware that as one channel closes, another one would open up.

The key elements to the Prison Service's Policy and Strategy on Drug Misuse and the three main areas of focus were:

1. reducing the supply of drugs
2. reducing the demand for drugs in the prison and rehabilitating drug misusers
3. measures to reduce the potential for damage to the health of prisoners, staff and the wider community, arising from the misuse of drugs.

It appeared to outsiders that the emphasis for reducing supply was firmly on enforcement, primarily through the searching of visitors and prisoners, alongside disincentives to prisoners (closed visits etc.). Whilst recognising that searches had to be carried out, Lucy posed the question as to whether the current degree of searching and restrictions on visitors was justified by the amount of drugs coming in through such means: eg. nappies, babies' food and bottles, shoes etc. Visitors (especially children), were innocent people and should be treated with basic levels of dignity and respect.

She suggested that the current emphasis would be unlikely to achieve its goals. The main thrust of the strategy ought to be prevention in its broadest sense. In order to prevent drugs coming in, the Prison Service must understand the complexity of issues around *why* prisoners asked their families to bring drugs in and *why* some decided to do so.

Joanna Morgan then asked participants to consider the broader meaning of prevention to tease out some of the issues. It was evident from this that it was difficult for many participants to externalise their thinking beyond the prison environment and to think of prevention in other than practical terms. Joanna drew participants to realise that prevention had to include support and education.

She then moved to a role play enacted by three members of the group playing the following characters:

- Prisoner who is a non-drug user but is being press-ganged into getting heroin in to the prison
- Wife (also mother of 2 small children)
- Prison Officer on duty at visit time

There were two parts to the plot: firstly a telephone call from the prisoner to his wife asking her to bring the stuff in (listened in to by the prison officer); secondly the visit itself. The rest of the group were asked to observe the characters closely, noting the dynamics at play and the issues at stake. At the end of the role play, the group was asked for their thoughts on each of the characters to reveal the pressures on them and enable people to think about what support measures might be needed to address some of the problems. It was clear to all that the wife was caught in the middle, fearing for her husband's safety and wanting to help him out because of her love for him, but worried about getting caught and particularly concerned for her children (for whom the prisoner showed no regard). The Prison Officer was under pressure from his peers to be tough and get arrests whilst the prisoner himself was fearful of what his peers would do to him should his wife fail to deliver the drugs. The 'characters' also spoke about how they felt at the end of the visit.

Lucy then explained that it was the recognition of these issues that led the Federation to consider how families could be supported to prevent them bring drugs in to prison. One strategy was to implement a series of training courses run by ADFAM National for the staff and volunteers of Visitors' Centres. Three two-day courses had been run and the post-course evaluation revealed that participants had found them extremely beneficial. The evaluation also asked them to describe incidents that had arisen since then which related to drugs misuse. Examples of the replies received included:

- Families not knowing the prisoner was using drugs and concern that the prisoner had started using drugs in prison, both of which led to anxiety for families (especially parents).
- Partner being put under pressure to supply drugs because the prisoner was being threatened.
- Extreme distress over the presence of children when an arrest was made. There was no knowledge about what happened to the child on arrest. The issue of children present when an adult is searched.
- Parents being torn between obligations and love for their son/daughter in prison and their anger over what they've done and the distress it has caused the rest of the family.

In order to begin to address some of these problems Lucy touched briefly on a number of approaches the Prison Service might consider adopting:

- Improved understanding and co-operation between Visitors' Centres and Prisons
- Better training of prison officers to include an understanding of the complex dynamics at play in relationships where drugs are an issue
- Developing a set of guidelines for the treatment of children on visits to include searching procedures; identifying someone to take responsibility for children when an adult is searched; ensuring procedures are in place for caring for a child where the accompanying adult is arrested. Participants were reminded of the Prison Service's obligations under the Children Act & UN Convention of the Rights of the Child (both 1989 - extracts attached).
- Producing clear, user-friendly information for visitors on security, searches and the implications of being caught with drugs. It was suggested that a video could be produced and shown in Visitors' Centres or through Support Groups to prepare people. Visitors should also be given access to support and someone to talk to in confidence.

Finally, it was suggested that the Prison Service develop a strategy built on the principle of prevention and acknowledging that families are innocent people whose support and co-operation is of vital importance to prisons. This could include:

- Placing the emphasis of intensive searching on the prisoner
- Only punishing the visitor (eg. with a closed visit) if it is known that they have brought in illicit goods
- Providing somewhere for visitors to safely dispose of drugs before entering the prison
- Considering a situation where prisons and families could work together to reduce harm and achieve the Service's aims eg. a visitor is unable to resist the psychological/emotional demands put on them and agrees to bring drugs in; on arrival however, they are able to have the drugs discovered on them at a search (having given prior warning) without fear of prosecution, yet in the knowledge that the prisoner would know she/he had attempted to bring it in.

———————— ● ————————

Children's Rights relevant to their treatment by the Prison Service

The UN Convention on the Rights of the Child, adopted in November 1989, stipulates that the State has an obligation to protect children from any form of discrimination or punishment *"on the basis of the status, (or) activities... of the child's parents, legal guardians or family members."*

Specifically Article 9 of the Convention declares that: *"States Parties shall respect the right of the child who is separated from one or both parents to maintain personal relations and direct contact with both parents on a regular basis, except if it is contrary to the child's best interests".*

The Department of Health's Regulations & Guidance underpinning the Children Act (1989) states vis a vis prison that: *"Family links should be actively maintained through visits and other forms of contact. Both parents are important even if one of them is no longer in the family home and fathers should not be overlooked or marginalised".*

The statement also recognises that *"continuity of relationships is important and attachments should be respected, sustained and developed"* whatever the cause of the separation.

The Children Act (1989) itself recognised that *"since discrimination of all kinds is an everyday reality in many children's lives, every effort must be made to ensure that agency services and practices do not reflect or reinforce it"*.

FOREIGN NATIONALS IN UK PRISONS
THE ROLE OF FPWP & HIBISCUS
Olga Heaven, Director, Female Prisoners'
Welfare Project/Hibiscus

The Female Prisoners' Welfare Project (FPWP) was established in 1986 to provide support for women prisoners of all ethnic origins and nationalities. Hibiscus (named after the tropical flower) was set up in 1991 to address the special needs of foreign women imprisoned in the United Kingdom. It is a branch of the FPWP organisation.[1] It has offices in Lagos, Nigeria and in Kingston, Jamaica.

Home Office Statistics indicate that approximately a quarter of women in prison are from ethnic minorities as against just 5% of the general population. Afro-Caribbeans and Africans are predominant in the ethnic minority population of the prisons, although they constitute just about 1.6% of the general population. The Hood Report[2], commissioned by the Commission for Racial Equality (CRE) and supported by the Lord Chancellor's office, detected significant racial discrimination in sentencing decisions. The narrowness of its remit precluded consideration of wider social economic and political aspects. Institutional racism, family structure, poor housing, poverty, unemployment and xenophobia were not considered. These wider economic, social and cultural differences, beyond the remit of the Hood Report, make "offending" more likely, arrest more frequent, sentencing harsher and treatment in prison less humane, for women as well as men.

The problems are far worse for blacks who are foreign nationals, especially those who import class A drugs such as cocaine and heroin. Their race, sex, nationality, poverty and isolation make them vulnerable to the worst forms of stereotyping and scape-goating. Gender based features such as concealment of drugs in the genitalia make for sensational tabloid treatment, whilst the higher class and educational attainments of male couriers give men a better chance of lower sentences. While the focus is on female couriers, there were only 214 females among 1059 foreign nationals in prison for drug offences in 1994. In 1990, there were 184 out of 1243, in 1991 181 out of 1063, in 1992 161 out of 1003 and in 1993 197 out of 991. In general, women carry much smaller quantities (100-500 gms) than men and so are responsible for a tiny fraction of the huge UK market.

Because of the sensational treatment of their cases, foreign women, especially black , now constitute a very significant proportion of the 1990 women in UK prisons; 30% of the population are foreign and 25% are black. The role of these women as scapegoats means that their cases are treated with less sympathy and objectivity. The stereotype of the female courier is of a beautiful greedy, sophisticated young woman who takes up this unpleasant trade to fuel a jet set lifestyle, including recreational drug use. However, research conducted by Dr Penny Green, amongst others, reveals typically an unemployed, middle aged, naive, poorly educated woman with an average of 3.5 children[3]. The women did not themselves take drugs and were often ignorant of their nature. Far from fuelling an affluent lifestyle most were on trying to raise school fees for their children or small capital for their businesses. Over 90% had children, and many were sole providers as single mothers, divorcees or widows; over half were unemployed, or poorly employed, and the vast majority came from countries suffering severe economic crisis[4].

Nigeria and Jamaica, which top the list of foreign nationals in prisons for drug offences, are classic examples. Home Office statistics indicate that in 1990, 83 of the 164 female foreign nationals in UK prisons were Nigerians and 30 Jamaicans. In 1991, the figures were 56 and 32 out of 141, in 1992 60 and 33 out of 131, in 1993 62 and 45 out of 183 and in 1994 49 and 46 out of 179. These women had particular problems which weighed the scales of justice against them within the system. Although English is the official language of Nigeria, it is not the first language for many of its varied communities. Many do not speak it at all, and most women couriers do not speak it well. English is the national language of Jamaica, but women with poor educational backgrounds, as most of the couriers are, would not easily be understood by the officers speaking any of the English dialects of the United Kingdom.

Many of these women were travelling abroad for the first time, and had not intended to stay more than a few days at most, as they had left many dependants behind, (over 90% have children). They were frightened, disoriented often poorly dressed for the climate, and sometimes ill from swallowing the drugs they transported. They were unaware of their rights and incapable of enforcing them since they were non-citizens and without the means of employing a counsel. Most were dissatisfied with the counsel provided, who appeared to assume they were guilty. Also bail was a problem as most had no one to stand surety, and there was the fear that they would abscond. Many of the women claimed they were duped, and that they were unaware they were carrying drugs.

Before Hibiscus was founded there were no Pre-Sentence Reports (PSR's) to help pleas for mitigation. In fact mitigation was problematic; since drug barons tend to choose mature decent women who have children in order to avoid detection, deterrence would be lost if decency and maturity were accepted as mitigating factors. In any event, Lord Lane's guideline of 1982 appears to have established minimal sentences based on the value of drugs: 4 years for any quantity, 7 years for any amount worth over one hundred thousand pounds, and 12-14 years for a million pounds plus. Without mitigating circumstances, these guidelines were more rigid for foreign nationals, and the high profile of their cases made "tough" sentencing acceptable as a deterrent. But much tougher sentences, including the death penalty at one time, did not seem to deter Nigerians. Although many of the women were first time offenders, their sentences averaged over six years. In prison there was little possibility of parole because Home Circumstances Reports, which are necessary for parole, were not available to foreign nationals.

As institutions of "punishment" prisons are not supposed to be easy, but to be effective in a human context, punishment must be humane, in order not to degrade or dehumanise. Cruel, inhuman punishment is universally condemned. Foreign nationals are isolated since they are spread over many prisons, with little or no contact with people from their own countries or communities. Their families are thousand of miles away and over the years many lose contact, due to illiteracy, lack of telephones and other means of communication. Their dependants, including young children, suffer, and the stress of not knowing what is happening to them is additional punishment. Their countries lack systems of care and social welfare, while families, which used to perform these roles, tend to disintegrate under stress of social economic, political and cultural pressure. Many women come to this country with a single change of clothes, if any, and they lack the means of clothing themselves in prison. Many cannot receive adequate health care, even where it is available, because due to cultural differences they may express their symptoms in language health personnel cannot understand. For Nigerians there is the additional fear of deportation after serving their sentences. Because of Decree 33 of October 1990; they could be jailed again on their return home as a result of being caught and sentenced outside Nigeria.

No one can reasonably argue that women who have been found guilty of drug offences should not be punished; but punishment needs to be fair as well as humane. It must be seen to "fit the crime". Fairness and equality are lost if prisoners suffer more or less due to nationality, race or ethnicity rather than degree of criminality.

Public Enlightenment

One of the principal ways of achieving the objectives of Hibiscus and its parent organisation, FPWP, is to enlighten the public about the special problems faced by foreign nationals and other women in UK prisons. Another is education of the women themselves about the harm they do, not only to themselves and to society but through the repercussions on their own families, through their involvement in the drug trade. "Tough" sentencing, meant to deter, fails among other reasons because potential couriers are unaware of the hazards they face with customs, police, courts and prison.

FPWP and Hibiscus workers give constant interviews and participate in seminars and conferences in the UK and abroad, and meet regularly with prisoners to discuss their problems and seek solutions. Hibiscus Jamaica organised a Drug Trafficking Prevention Seminar which took place in Kingston on the 31st October 1995. This was heavily publicised with the use of graphic posters. Many major organisations were involved, and plans are under-way to organise similar projects in other major cities. The national media have shown great interest because drug abuse is a very serious problem in Jamaica. The playwright Winsome Pinnock consulted Hibiscus Jamaica during research for her play 'Mules', which was shown in London in May 1996 and was reviewed by the BBC World Service on 10th May 1996.

The most successful promotion of FPWP and Hibiscus so far has been a documentary, also called 'Mules', made by Olivia Liechtenstein in 1992 for BBC 1 television. The thirty minute film focused on the problems of Nigerian women imprisoned for importing drugs into the United Kingdom, and the role of Hibiscus assisting them. It covered the activities of the Hibiscus office in Lagos and interviewed Nigerian government officials. Experts, such as Helena Kennedy QC, highlighted the problems faced by these women in the UK criminal justice system.

After the programme was shown, the FPWP and Hibiscus office in the UK was overwhelmed by requests for more information and offers of assistance. The Home Office and judiciary consulted on a more regular basis, and made greater use of Hibiscus resources in providing Pre-Sentence and Home Circumstances Reports, and the women themselves were given a moral booster by having their problems aired.

The largest impact was felt however, in Nigeria, where the film was broadcast on national television from a recording by the Nigerian High Commission in London. For the first time many potential couriers saw in graphic detail the horrors in store in the United Kingdom for those caught carrying drugs. More importantly, the military dictatorship, sensitive to charges that it was "soft" on drugs (if not actually involved in the trade) was so embarrassed that it took defensive action to improve its enforcement policy.

The National Drug Law Enforcement Agency (NDLEA), which has been involved in spectacular scandals in the past, was overhauled and new leadership appointed. "Businessmen" and women were forced to account for assets, including expensive cars. Money laundering was attacked, and drug suspects were not just arrested but tried and convicted, instead of disappearing with their drugs after bribing officials. Since Nigeria does not produce the drugs it re-exports to the UK and other countries, the NDLEA now demand clearance from all Nigerians planning to travel to drug-producing countries such as Pakistan, Thailand and Iran.

Newswatch magazine of 29th April 1996 reported that in 1994, 640 people were arrested with 203 million Naira (approx. 1.65 million pounds) worth of drugs. In 1995 798 were arrested, and by January 1996, 333 of these had been convicted. According to the Middlesex Probation Service Foreign Nationals Unit, using Home Office statistics from the S2 Division, the number of Nigerians sentenced for drug offences in the UK fell from 63 in 1990 to 39 in 1994. Ironically Hibiscus, an organisation set up to mitigate the harsh sentencing policy of a misguided and ineffective deterrent strategy, may have given the policy its only success by enlightening the Nigerian public about the fate of its drug couriers, and the Nigerian regime about the harm its tolerance of the drug trade does to its image.

Conclusion: Problems and Prospects

So far Hibiscus has achieved many of its objectives, and has given very good value for its money. On a budget of approximately £25,000 it has run offices employing many staff in two foreign countries, supplying relief to foreign nationals in prison as well as to their dependants in Nigeria and Jamaica and supplying Pre-Sentence and Home Circumstances Reports to help the judiciary and the Home Office to be fairer and more effective in sentencing and parole. The organisation's success in enlightening the public of the evil consequences of the drug trade, has also helped to reduce the number of offenders, thus reducing the demand on its services for welfare.

The hope of all charities is that the suffering they exist to help alleviate will disappear, making their existence unnecessary. However, as long as suffering exists, organisations such as FPWP and Hibiscus will soldier on. The social economic, political and cultural conditions that create the problems which we have attempted to describe in this paper, will be with us for a long time. Hibiscus must therefore consolidate the modest gains it has made, and look to expand in the future, especially to other parts of West Africa and South America, the homes of a significant proportion of the total of women prisoners in UK prisons.

Notes
1. For background on Hibiscus, see the Annual Report of FPWP and Hibiscus, and "Hibiscus working with Nigerian Women Prisoners" by Olga Heaven in "Drug Couriers" edited by Penny Green.
2. The Hood Report, by Roger Hood, published by Clarendon Press as "Race and Sentencing: A Study in the Crown Court", summarised by the Commission for Racial Equality under "A Question of Judgement". See also, "The Sentencing of Drug Couriers" by Rudi Foreson, in Penny Green (ed.), op cit.
3. For an account of stereotyping see "Drug Couriers: Construction of a Public Enemy" by Penny Green (ed.) ibid.
4. For social background of couriers see Penny Green; ibid., and the Annual Report of Hibiscus.

Hibiscus may be contacted c/o FPWP at 15 Great St Thomas Apostle, London EC4V 2BB.

DRUG INTERVENTIONS IN THE CRIMINAL JUSTICE SYSTEM
A SOUTH LONDON STRATEGY

Jud Barker, Team Leader, Home Office
Drugs Prevention Team in South London

In late 1994, in Leicester, the Home Office Drugs Prevention Initiative organised, sponsored and ran a National Working Seminar whose attendees represented criminal justice, specialist drugs, local authority and other agencies from all over England. Delegates included frontline drugs workers, police and probation officers, Crown Prosecutors, defence lawyers, forensic medical examiners, prison officials, members of Local Authority Social Services, Community Safety and Housing Departments, and members of the magistracy and judiciary, to name but a few.

The Leicester seminar was called *Drugs Prevention in the Criminal Justice System*. Its aim was to identify principles on which to base guidelines for good practice in providing helping interventions for drug users and those at risk who come into contact with the criminal justice system.

At the end of the seminar, the Drugs Prevention Initiative (DPI) undertook to draft and circulate guidelines based on delegates' conclusions. The DPI further undertook to test these guidelines in two or three major demonstration projects in different areas of the country covered by Local Drugs Prevention Teams during Phase 2 of the DPI, which runs from April 1995 to March 1999.

The South London Strategy is one of three such projects which have since been set up specifically to honour the Drugs Prevention Initiative's undertaking at the Leicester seminar. Two other Local Team - sponsored projects are also being evaluated within the DPI's corporate Adult Criminal Justice Drugs Interventions programme.

I propose to describe the three year South London project, its aim and objectives, how we are attempting or propose to meet and measure these objectives and how, in the process, the project sets out to test the Leicester seminar's guidelines.

Before I do this, however, I would like to do two things. Firstly, I would like to emphasise that the strategy in South London is an ambitious and complex experiment which is, at this stage in the game, fairly early on in its progress. At its heart, the project seeks to marry up what - in England, anyway - has been the historically contrasting (dare I say often conflicting) criminal justice and welfare approaches to working with people who misuse drugs. This is a pretty tall order in itself and as a consequence, quite frankly, I am not completely sure yet how - never mind if - the experiment, with all its various components, will work.

Secondly, I want to tell you something of why I, personally, really want the experiment to work. I would like to do this by taking you through a case I became involved in, a while back, when I worked at the London Borough of Southwark's Drugs Misuse Unit. It is an experience which I have to admit has been a major reference point for me, and given the high falutin' nature of the South London Strategy. Maybe it will be a good way to help keep our discussions here today well grounded in reality.

Karen's Story

No matter how flawed we may find, think or have experienced our criminal justice system to be - and I, for one, have no doubt that it is flawed - it is still one of the most steadfast, if not the oldest, of our social institutions which, at least, strives to balance the rights and needs and safety of the larger community and the rights, needs, safety and civil liberties of the individual.

In my experience, if there was ever a social issue to test the aspirations of this institution - to measure public safety against personal choice - drugs misuse is it. I think that Karen's story, and some admittedly subjective conclusions drawn from it, serve poignantly to illustrate the point.

Karen's story begins more than eight years ago and, as you will hear, it is a story with many characters. The central characters, however, are:

- Karen, herself, a middle aged, single mother of a large immediate and much larger extended family;
- Karen's teenage daughter who is dependent on heroin and other drugs;
- Karen's daughter's partner who is also a drug addict and a major local street level drugs dealer; and,

- the couple's baby, Karen's eighteen month old grand daughter.

On an evening almost exactly eight years ago, I was at home looking after my own two small children when I received a telephone call - around 9pm - from Karen.

She was someone with whom I had been working for over a year. She had come to our Unit seeking practical help for dealing with the problems which her daughter's and son-in-law's drugs misuse were creating for her. Even then, Karen feared desperately for her daughter, for her grand daughter, for herself and the rest of her family.

The couple's drugs related activities had directly affected Karen and her family in many ways:
- there were numerous threats to the family, at all times of the night and day, by people unknown to Karen - people seeking retribution from the couple for certain 'unpaid bills';
- a car was set alight in the early hours of the morning outside the family home;
- a gun was found in the bedside table of the daughter's room in the family home;
- a large quantity of drugs left in the daughter's handbag was found by Karen who took it upon herself to get rid of the drugs - with awful consequences when her son-in-law, upset by the loss of his stash, viciously attacked Karen's daughter and hurt her grand daughter in the cross fire;
- on one of the many times the couple were arrested, Karen refused to stand bail, and paid the price when her son-in-law sent his friends around to harass and admonish her for failing in her 'duties as a mother'.

By the time Karen came to me, she was seeking help to find housing away from the area - away from the couple and their connections - and to help her in her efforts to gain custody of her baby grand daughter.

Whilst Karen and I worked together on these specific needs, her daughter and son-in-law were arrested for fire arms offences. He was charged, remanded in custody and when he appeared in court on the charge, Karen's daughter was caught supplying him with drugs and syringes. Karen's daughter was subsequently remanded in custody. Her son-in-law was convicted on the fire arms charge and sent to prison. From prison, he ensured that the couple's local allies regularly reminded Karen that he would oppose any of her efforts to gain custody of the baby for whom, by this time, she had been caring for most of the child's life.

Over time, arrangements through the local authority, for rehousing the family failed. An attempt to arrange a house swap through a local voluntary organisation also came to nothing. Karen's daughter came and went, insistent on her mother's help to pull her out of her bouts with the criminal justice system - and once out, unable and unwilling to stay away from the father of her child, in spite of his incarceration and conditions placed on her own probation order.

Karen and her family were besieged. Karen was despairing and sometimes terribly ambivalent. She felt responsible for and guilty about the actions of her daughter, reluctant to abandon her and at the same time furious that her daughter should so abuse her, make so many demands on her. And she had the rest of her family (including her own two children under ten, and an older son who was particularly targeted by the couple's local lackeys) to consider. She would disappear for days, taking her family with her to secret places, emerging eventually to meet up with me or to bring her daughter clean clothes at whatever prison or hostel her daughter happened at the time to be remanded to.

Karen was physically and emotionally trapped, utterly exhausted and apparently totally unable to find any way out of her dilemma. In fact, we were to learn later from a psychiatrist who interviewed her, she was to all intents and purposes, 'shellshocked' - beaten down by the unrelenting threatened and actual violence to which she and her family were subjected for so long. This was how profoundly Karen - someone who had nothing to do with drugs - was touched by the personal choices and actions of those who did.

The night Karen rang me, she did so to tell me that she had just murdered her son-in-law. She said that she had 'stabbed and stabbed' him and that she had hit him on the head 'over and over again'. She left the telephone three times to see if he was dead... and returned each time to ask me how long it takes for someone to die. She kept repeating that she had committed a mortal sin. I rang the police and whilst we waited for their arrival, we talked as she sipped a cup of tea, chatting childlike with a dreadfully tenuous calm, about nothing in particular.

That night, and in the events that followed, I learned all too dramatically, about the impact of an individual's drugs misuse on other people - the imposition of what had started out as personal choice (and there is no other name for it) on those, as it would transpire, who were not yet even able to make choices of any kind.

It was to be a year later that I saw Karen again when she appeared at the Old Bailey and at the last minute pleaded guilty to a reduced charge of manslaughter on the grounds of diminished responsibility. The judge took a full day to decide upon her sentence. I will always remember clearly - and I have to say with great admiration - how he grappled with all the underlying issues and inter-related events underpinning and leading up to the one desperate, horrific and irredeemable act of the defendant. Each one of us who appeared as expert witnesses were asked, among others, the same question - 'have the circumstances which led to this terrible thing changed: has this woman's daughter stopped using drugs?'

In the end, Karen received a two year probation order with condition. But that was not the end of the story by a long shot. The condition of her probation order was that she and her grand daughter, for whom Karen had by this stage obtained custody, regularly attended psychiatric sessions as the child grew older. This was to prepare in the long term for the child's eventually learning and coping with the realisation that her grandmother - the woman who had cared and nurtured and mothered and protected her for most of her life - was also the convicted killer of her father.

Could it all have been prevented? I wondered this as I sat there listening to the judge struggle with all the considerations which he must take into account in deciding whether to spare Karen a custodial sentence. Look at all the clues and indications so many of us had over so long a period, of things going terribly wrong. Look along the way at all the agencies that had been involved, all the resources spent by: social services, housing, the courts, the CPS, the police, the probation service, lawyers, the medical profession, my own local authority based unit. What if we had been able to intervene sooner? What if we had been able to pick up Karen's daughter and her drug use, say...

- before, or at least, when her child was born
- the time her mother went to the police station with a handbag full of drugs
- the time the housing department was called out to a domestic dispute at the local authority run hostel where Karen's daughter and son-in-law lived with their baby
- the first, indeed, second, third or fourth time she was arrested
- when she was remanded in custody
- when she was on probation, breaching her conditions left, right and centre.

There were so many of us professional agencies dealing, in one way or another, directly or indirectly, to a greater or lesser degree, with Karen's daughter over a period of at least two years.

Would it have made a difference if we had been able to work more closely together? Had better coordinated our professional aims and efforts? Had organised ourselves around the myriad needs of the individual characters in this story - our prisoners, clients, defendants, patients, tenants, consumers (whatever we deem to call them) - rather than leaving it to them, in one form or another, to shop around taking whatever our limited, unrelated and uncoordinated professionally defined boundaries allowed us to give them at the time?

Would it have meant one less drug user; one less violent death; one less convicted killer; one less baby born into a pain and trauma she has not chosen and perhaps has no means to cope with; one less next generation teenager with a damn good reason for using drugs to distance herself from the pain?

Would it have made a difference if we professionals had worked differently?

I don't know... but therein lies the overall aim of the South London Strategy: "To determine whether preventive and helping interventions at various points of contact within the criminal justice system can be effective in reducing drugs misuse and related offending."

The South London Strategy
[A complete South London Strategy document which includes a summary of the Leicester Guidelines can be obtained from the South London Drugs Prevention Team.]

THE CATCHMENT AREA

The South London Strategy covers the five inner London boroughs of Wandsworth, Lambeth, Southwark, Lewisham and Greenwich. This area represents a total population of some 1.2 million and contains within it some of the most deprived inner cities areas to be found in this country.

Having said this, local conditions and characteristics within as well as across the five boroughs are pretty diverse. Across the board, however, we are talking about:

- a population around 62% of which is of employable age
- an unemployment rate of 17% for men, and 11% for women (National Average 11% and 6.8% respectively - OPCS 1991)
- a non white population of 21% (5.5% National)
- an owner/occupier rate of 44% (66.4% National).

Drugs misuse, especially in the boroughs of Lambeth, Southwark and Lewisham (but increasingly now in the other two as well) is and has been endemic - a problem growing in prevalence and complexity since the early eighties. The area is relatively well served by established specialist drugs agencies - both voluntary and NHS - which is perhaps, in a twisted sort of way, one indication of the extent and history of drugs misuse in the locale.

1. STRATEGY AIM AND OBJECTIVES

OVERALL AIM:

To determine whether preventive and helping interventions at various points of contact within the criminal justice system can be effective in reducing drugs misuse and related offending.

OBJECTIVES:
- To test draft guidelines based on principles identified at the Leicester National Working Seminar held in late 1994;
- To provide a coordinated programme of preventive and helping interventions at all or several sequential points of contact within the criminal justice system from pre-prosecution to post prison release;
- To determine whether there is added value in an integrated system of interventions across the criminal justice system; and
- To lay the foundations for a national strategy for drugs interventions in the criminal justice system.

Leicester Seminar Guidelines: Aim and Objectives

On Definitions

"'Prevention' is the overall aim and is defined in its broadest sense. This includes: continued abstinence from drugs misuse; delayed onset; avoidance of escalation; or reduced misuse (including a return to abstinence)."

"'Intervention' is how the overall aim will be achieved, by providing information, advice, problem and needs assessment and programmes of help to people identified through their contact at various points within the criminal justice system."

On Local Project Structure

"To provide preventive and helping interventions, in a continuum, at as many points of contact with the CJS as possible from pre-prosecution to post prison release: ideally, at all points; at least, at several sequential points

2. SOUTH LONDON STRATEGY COMPONENTS

In South London we have opted to implement the seminar's recommendation for an 'ideal' or fully comprehensive programme of interventions.

Police referral	(i.e.on arrest)
Court referral	(i.e.before or on sentencing)
Probation referral	(i.e.whilst serving a community sentence)
Prison referral	(i.e.on remand or whilst serving a custodial sentence)
	(i.e. when released on licence or otherwise)

Leicester Seminar Guidelines: On Resources

"To, in the first instance, build on existing local good practice and better (more coordinated) use of resources identified in an initial audit of local services and initiatives."

With this in mind there are four components to the strategy. It is important to note that within most of these components, there is some form or level of relevant work already being done in some agencies. The strategy seeks therefore to:

- harness existing good practice and ensure its co-ordination with other similar good practice across the five boroughs;
- establish good practice where it does not yet exist; and,
- ensure that both existing and new work is coordinated in such a way as to provide for a continuum of interventions as set out in the Leicester seminar guidelines.

We are moving step by step in implementing the various components of the strategy, starting with police referral and working our way through to post prison release.

Police Referral

This is the most advanced part of the strategy with all twelve of the divisional police stations having agreed in practice or principle to hand out/display the publicity and make referrals. Six stations (in Lambeth and Southwark) are already operating the system and the other six are awaiting appointments of, or some temporary alternative arrangements for bringing on line specialist drugs agency input. An Arrest Referral Scheme has been operational, in one form or another, in Southwark since 1988 and the strategy uses this model for police stations in the other four boroughs.

Court Referral

We are currently devising a proposal for this component based on consultations with the Probation Service and Magistracy and Lay Justices at our three Magistrates Courts and one of the Crown Courts sited within the area.

Probation Referral

This component builds on fairly extensive existing good practice within our local field based probation offices. We are currently exploring how this can be better coordinated and how it can be integrated into and benefit from the strategy.

Prison Referral

Prison referral is the least advanced part of the strategy for a range of reasons, not least because of the national catchment areas prisons cover. At the moment we are preparing to consult with staff at two of the three prisons sited in the area to decide how best to develop this part of the strategy. We are currently making arrangements with the Throughcare Team at HMP Wandsworth to practically establish activities within the strategy which will complement and enhance the prison's current work with drug users.

KEY ELEMENTS FOR MEETING THESE AIMS AND OBJECTIVES

Project partnership	manages the strategy
Project team	provides initial interventions and, as necessary, ongoing key work
Project coordinator	coordinates strategy activities across five boroughs
Project publicity	improves access to help
Project evaluation	determines what works, what doesn't and why

It is important to emphasise that the South London Strategy is NOT a scheme which sets out to divert people from the criminal justice system. It is a project which targets those who are identified because of their contact with the CJS. It seeks to exploit potential incentives for drug users to take up help during, for example, the crises of arrest, court appearance or impending custodial sentence. A possible outcome, depending on the efforts of those who take up the scheme, may be an alternative to a custodial sentence.

3.   PROJECT PARTNERSHIP
- Responsible for managing the strategy's development, implementation, monitoring, problem solving and evaluation.
- Comprises management level representatives of local specialist drugs agencies, criminal justice agencies, local authority departments/community safety officers and others with a **vested interest** in the objectives and outcomes of the strategy.
- It is a requirement that managers of workers who make up the Project Team serve on the Project Partnership.
- Provided full time dedicated secretariat support by the South London Drugs Prevention Team.

Leicester Seminar Guidelines: On Partnership Membership and Support
"To select representatives of member agencies/organisations who are of sufficient existing or delegated authority within their organisations to ensure that their organisations' contributions to a corporate approach can be delivered."

"To ensure that working partnerships are adequately supported, ideally by some dedicated secretariat provision which both services the partnership group meetings and ensures that decisions of the group are carried out."

NOTES: Vested interest - to ensure that there is something significant in it for all the full time professionals who are volunteering their time to attend yet another meeting.

Project Team Manager attendance required - to ensure that workers' team efforts are in line, not in conflict, with the management and practices of the agencies by which they are employed.

The South London Partnership was formally established with 28 members in January 1996 with agreed terms of reference and an elected Chair and Vice Chair who are a stipendiary magistrate and local drug agency director respectively. It is envisaged that the membership will increase over time as the strategy develops.

4.   THE PROJECT TEAM
- Core group comprises specialist drugs workers who are, within their own agencies, dedicated Criminal Justice Liaison Workers (Ideally 2 such workers for each of the five boroughs)
- Drawn from existing local specialist drugs agencies which have agreed to second a proportion or all of their staff time to the Project Team and strategy objectives
- Equipped with mobile telephones and on-call to local police, courts, probation and prisons
- Provide initial client or agency needs assessment (common comprehensive assessment form)
- Arrange and as necessary take key role in coordinating appropriate longer term interventions including comprehensive programmes of help

[It is a requirement that the agency managers of these Project Team members serve on the Project Partnership.]

Leicester Seminar Guidelines: On Resources
"To, in the first instance, build on existing good practice and better (more coordinated) use of resources identified in an initial audit of local services and initiatives."

NOTE: The Project Team has been established with dedicated workers from agencies serving each of the five boroughs. Four of these are currently operational (equipped with mobile telephones and on call to their local police stations). An additional four are providing some temporary cover whilst the Drugs Prevention Team assists their agencies in funding and appointing dedicated staff. A voluntary agency

Court Advice Worker is online to make referrals from one of the local Magistrates' Courts. The existing Project Team members have volunteered to cover for each other until the full team complement of twelve workers (two for each borough) is met. Eventually, it is envisaged that the Project Team will include criminal justice agency fieldbased workers (for example police and probation officers) who initially identify and refer people to the project.

5.   PROJECT COORDINATOR
The Project Coordinator has been appointed and took up his post in July 1996.

- Coordinates the work of the Project Team across the strategy's five boroughs
- Promotes the strategy and ensures the decisions of the Project Partnership are carried out within and between participating local agencies
- Takes charge of and oversees a central 0800 helpline for people who refer themselves after being introduced to the project at their first point of contact with the criminal justice system
- Generally 'trouble-shoots' and advises the Project Partnership and the Project Team when frontline problems occur

Leicester Seminar Guidelines
"The Project Coordinator is to be based with the South London Drugs Prevention Team and contributes to the SLDPT's provision of full time dedicated secretariat support for the Project Partnership and the strategy in general."

6.   PROJECT PUBLICITY/QUICK ACCESS TO SERVICES
This involves an: 0800 helpline for self referral; posters/referral cards for participating CJS agencies; mobile telephones for drugs workers; immediate comprehensive assessment for clients who want the scheme.

7.   PROJECT EVALUATION
- Is built into the strategy from its outset
- Is undertaken by independent researchers
- Evaluates baseline, process and outcomes (including those who do not take up the project)
- Provides additional means for Project Partnership to monitor strategy and address problems and issues that arise in the course of the project - ie. action/research
- By 1999 tells us what works, what does not and why and assists in laying the groundwork for a national strategy

Leicester Seminar Guidelines
"To ensure that from the outset of project planning, arrangements are made for credible evaluation of the project and, in this, the realism of project aim and objectives is measured by their ability to be evaluated."

The South London Strategy is one of five DPI projects (three demonstration projects) subject to independent evaluative research commissioned by our Central Unit's Research Section. Professor Mike Hough, from the South Bank University, and his team are conducting the research.

Because of the size and complexity of the South London project, Mike has proposed a 'sampling' approach which focuses on one local police station per borough and its 'criminal justice and drug agency family'. The Research Team is currently piloting this approach at a divisional police station in Lambeth. Recent feedback from the Research Team has already proved useful to the Partnership's efforts to monitor and improve the project as it progresses.

The South London Drugs Prevention Team may be contacted at County House, 190 Great Dover Street, London SE1 4YB.

MEDICAL CONTRIBUTIONS TO THE MANAGEMENT OF THE DRUG ABUSE PROBLEM
Dr Vanessa Crawford, Clinical Lecturer in Addictive Behaviour, St George's Hospital Medical School

Tackling Drugs Together in Clinical Practice

The Department of Addictive Behaviour at St George's Hospital provides a vast range of services aiming to ensure that substance misusers, a heterogeneous population, have a service which is appropriate to their needs. Service provision is backed up by education and research.

St George's Hospital serves the boroughs of Merton, Sutton and Wandsworth and the South Thames (West) Area. The service is constantly being assessed to ensure that it is meeting the needs of those it is there to serve. This has led to the current reconfiguration of services to provide a Borough focused approach.

Clinical Services
The In-Patient Treatment Unit

The Unit is a tertiary referral service housing a 12 bedded acute facility and a 'recovery' ward providing 11 beds and 12 day places.

The unit aims to assess the physical, psychological and social needs of drug dependent patients and to offer suitable treatment and rehabilitation. The majority of admissions have primary opiate problems, but many are also dependent on benzodiazepines and/or alcohol. Stimulant users are also admitted. Treatment involves assessment of dependence, observation for withdrawal symptoms followed by stabilisation and detoxification. Patients on opiates generally elect to undergo a standard reduction methadone programme, but some may specifically request a non-opiate detoxification.

The patients undergo a physical examination on the day of admission. They are offered the opportunity to have a routine blood screen and testing for Hepatitis B, C and HIV with pre-test counselling. HIV testing can be done in the Genito-urinary medicine clinic if the patient would prefer their status to be confidential to them and the clinic. In view of the high prevalence of Hepatitis C within the population we see, we need to become more aware of there being a psycho-social impact potentially similar to that of testing HIV positive. Admitting a person gives an excellent opportunity to also make a full assessment of their mental state, particularly once they have detoxified from all medication.

The ultimate responsibility for each patient is held by the two consultants in charge of the ward. There are two ward rounds held each week. One is a management round, in which all patients are reviewed and the second is an in-depth study which involves a multi-disciplinary review of three patients each week.

The timetable for the patients is a combination of group work and one to one supportive counselling. There is the opportunity for psychological assessment and input for all patients; again this needs to be tailored to the needs of the individual. The aim is for patients to have organised rehabilitation and funding prior to admission.

The Drug Dependency Unit

The outpatient clinic has been established since 1967. Although the clinic has never been 'substance specific', the patients who attend are predominantly those who are opiate dependent or have mixed dependencies. Considerable emphasis is placed on in-depth assessment, using a multidisciplinary team. Treatment interventions include both pharmacological and psychosocial treatment.

The Regional Drug and Alcohol Team

Set up in the late 1980s, this team provides a wide range of services to the South Thames (West) area. The multidisciplinary team, with experienced personnel from health, psychology, social work, research and information science background enables an integrated and multifaceted approach.

One of the roles of the RDAT is in the area of needs assessment. Needs assessment in the substance misuse field is a complex area as substance misusers are not a highly evident, accessible, homogenous group. The team can give advice and assistance in carrying out needs assessment and on appropriate service configuration. RDAT also aims to disseminate information on good practice and models of intervention from advice and counselling through to recovery/rehabilitation programmes and inter-agency collaboration. RDAT provide independent advice through audit to look at cost effective service provision. They can advise on business planning, marketing and submitting bids and funding proposals. The team provides support for and facilitates education and training activities throughout the South Thames (West) area for drug and alcohol workers. The team also provides a tertiary referral clinical service, assessing drug users referred by drug services in South Thames (West). Most are referred for assessment for admission to the In-patient Unit at Springfield University Hospital, but some are referred for advice on management. The assessment is carried out by 2 team members which proves to be very useful in formulating the case.

Drug and Alcohol Liaison Team (DALT)
Why should we offer this service to the general hospital wards, particularly when there is already a general psychiatry liaison service? The service is offered on the basis of research which includes the following:

Patients admitted with direct consequences of consumption:
27% of emergency medical admissions (Lockhart, 1986)
26% of patients admitted at night were drunk (Glynn & O'Neill, 1974)

Patients admitted with direct consequences of misuse:
30% of acute hospital admissions have alcohol problems (Tomlinson, 1992)
26% of male medical in-patients with alcohol problems (Quinn and Johnston, 1976)
27% of male medical in-patients were problem drinkers (Lloyd et al, 1982)

Substance misuse problems are found to be most common among medical, surgical and orthopaedic patients and least common among gynaecology, ENT, dental and plastic surgery.

DALT offers a weekday service to the general hospital wards. In particular assessment of drug and alcohol problems and advice and guidance pertaining to substance use, consequences and treatment options. In conjunction with the referring team, DALT will liaise with and refer on to other drug/alcohol agencies both statutory and non-statutory. The service also offers professional support, advice and guidance to ward staff.

Addiction Prevention in Primary Care
The Addiction Prevention in Primary Care Programme began as a 3 year rolling programme in September 1991 as a 3 year joint project between the Department of Addictive Behaviour at St George's Hospital Medical School and Merton, Sutton and Wandsworth Family Health Service Authority. The team of three Addiction Prevention Counsellors (APCs) go out to and work within General Practice to promote the early recognition of and intervention in substance misuse problems by Primary Health Care Staff (PHC). Each counsellor covers one of the three boroughs; each is attached to a base practice where they offer an on-going clinical service for at least one year. All other practices are offered a clinical service for between three and six months.

As about 90% of the practice population visit the GP within any three year period, there are many opportunities to influence a large number of patients. The APCs aim to facilitate the PHC staff in the early recognition of and intervention in the problems associated with substance use and misuse. The programme covers all classes of psycho-active substances and includes alcohol and tobacco. The main aim of the project is to equip the PHC staff with the necessary skills, knowledge and confidence to enable them to work effectively in this field.

Shared Care
Given the role of the General Practitioner as the primary carer good communication between drug services and GPs is essential. Substance misusers still provide a great deal of concern to the majority of GPs; there is a fear of the surgery being over run by disruptive, manipulative patients who will take up too much time and disturb the 'other' patients. There has been a failure to accept that substance misuse and dependence covers a wide range, so that all GPs have substance misusers on their lists but may fail to recognise them or choose not to unearth them. Much of this is through fear and feeling deskilled. In addition, to date there has been no financial incentive to address these problems.

There is a need for the substance misuse services to improve communication and liaison with primary care in order to facilitate and support their increased input. Substance misuse services can help the GP to identify the extent to which the individual patients can be managed in primary care.

The Substance Use Database

The substance use database is part of a national initiative to monitor problem drug use within the community. In October 1989, the Department of Health distributed a circular, asking Regional Health Authorities 'to set up a database to monitor trends in drug misuse and the use of drug misuse services'. The circular also requested that systems be developed for providing this information to the Department of Health.

Prior to the establishment of the Regional Databases, the lack of information about trends in the extent and nature of drug misuse, made it extremely difficult to plan and provide relevant services. The Department of Addictive Behaviour at St George's Hospital has been working for some years on the development of a concise and efficient database. The SAAQ records data gathered at an in-depth interview with each patient and can be used for clinical and research purposes. The Substance Use Database (SUD) form is a one page precis of the essential items from the SAAQ.

As well as collecting data to comply with the Department of Health, SUD is also useful as a tool to individual agencies, purchasers and service planners. The database in South West Thames is unique in also collecting data on alcohol as a main substance of use.

Education and Training

All members of the department are involved in education and training. The department runs courses in Addictive Behaviour, from Certificate through Diploma to MSc level, for all disciplines from statutory and non statutory services. Unfortunately one of the hardest courses to recruit for is in the Diploma in Addictive Behaviour for General Practitioners. All courses aim to influence the participants' knowledge, skills and attitudes. Great emphasis is placed on the training of medical students. The majority of today's doctors had very little, if any, training in Addictive Behaviour.

Research

The department has the privilege of access to material for research. Much work is being done on the factors which influence outcome, in order to tailor the service to produce the best outcome for the patient. Research has been carried out on the incidence of personality disorder on admission to the inpatient unit. The 6 month follow up is now coming to an end and the data is being analysed to look at outcome. In addition, we are looking at the incidence of dual diagnosis; again to look at the impact on outcome and the possible need to tailor service provision accordingly. The need to assess opiate dependence and instigate treatment as soon as possible is essential; the use of naloxone eye drops as a test of opiate addiction is currently under review.

Audit

Hepatitis B vaccination programme

The Hepatitis B vaccination programme was introduced in September 1994. Vaccination is recommended for individuals at high risk of contracting Hepatitis B infection, through drug use and/or sexual transmission, who meet the following criteria:

* Patients whose past or present drug use includes parenteral route of administration.
* Patients who are using potentially injectable drugs, even if there is no history of parenteral use.
* Patients who have a sexual partner who is a drug abuser.
* Patients who are or have been involved in prostitution, and bisexual or homosexual males.
* Other patients who request vaccination will be considered on an individual basis.

The standards set are as follows:

* all patients are given information about Hepatitis B at the earliest opportunity
* Hepatitis B core antibody status will normally be ascertained before beginning vaccination by means of a blood test
* positive encouragement should be given to patients to accept vaccination as a safe preventative health measure
* each treatment team to develop an appropriate system for maintaining records, and for following up patients
* for in-patients who commence vaccination, the referring team and follow up agency must be informed of the next due dose on discharge.

Results
Of a total of 192 admissions from 1 January 1995-31 December 1995, 17 were re-admissions and a total of 101 patients (53%) consented to the Hepatitis B vaccination programme. Of the 101 patients who consented:
2 did not have a blood test
94 had a Hepatitis B core antibody negative result
4 had a Hepatitis B core antibody positive result (immune)
1 had a Hepatitis B surface antigen positive result (carrier)
3 patients refused vaccination
91 started their programme

Drug Dependency Unit
The programme was introduced in May 1995 and audited in January 1996 to determine the completion rate and effectiveness (ie the development of immunity, the number of new cases of Hepatitis B)
All individuals who commenced vaccination programmes in May-July 1995 should have completed the course (3 injections - at 0 month, 1 month and 6 months)
Results
Number commencing the programme in May-July 1995 = 20
Number who completed programme = 14 (70%)
Number of defaulters = 6 (30%) 1 in prison
Number of letters sent to eligible defaulters = 5 (100%)
Only 1 so far has been eligible for post vaccination serology
All GPs were informed

Follow up must attempt to ensure that 2nd and 3rd doses are given, by sending letters to the patient and their GP. The outcome of post vaccination serology can be checked at month 8.

Community Alcohol Team (CAT)
The CAT looked at the number of referrals across the 3 Boroughs they cover, breaking them down by postcode, to ensure that the distribution of staff across the Boroughs was uniform.
An audit of ethnicity by area of residence has been carried out as it is often claimed that problem drinkers from ethnic minority groups (particularly Asian and African or Caribbean) find difficulty in accessing conventional specialist psychiatric services and may require special services to cater to their particular needs.
Findings
N = 450 clients seen over an 18 month period
399 = white (88.7%)
51 = ethnic minority (11.3%)

The proportion of ethnic minority clients compared with white clients was not significantly different from the proportion found in the general population in each of the three Boroughs. Further there were few differences in other characteristics between the ethnic and white samples in relation to drinking history. Where differences were found, they tended to suggest that the white group had more problems of longer duration than the ethnic group.

Conclusion
The medical profession is in a privileged position to influence the setting up and running of services within the field of substance misuse. The physician can only fulfil this role with the full support of a multidisciplinary team. It is the responsibility of the physician to ensure good clinical practice and to disseminate this information to colleagues within other medical specialities. Services need to be flexible to the needs of their clients and the ever changing pattern of drug misuse. In addition to providing a clinical service, research, audit and education should be an integral part of all addiction services.

MAD, BAD AND UNSAFE? THE EFFECTS OF DRUG USE ON SEXUAL BEHAVIOUR
Tim Rhodes, Research Fellow, Centre for Research on Drugs & Health Behaviour

Do drugs have 'disinhibitive' effects?

There are probably a few people in Britain today who would doubt that alcohol has 'disinhibitive' effects, particularly as far as sexual behaviour is concerned. Our research confirms that the same is true of some other drugs, particularly stimulants. As commented by a user of ecstasy: "It definitely makes me more confident [and] lose all my inhibitions", and a user of cocaine: "It takes away a lot of inhibitions obviously, and sexually it does do that as well you know."

The disinhibitive effects of alcohol and stimulants were seen to make the initiation of sexual encounters easier. These effects ranged from casual eye-contact to flirtation. They were also seen to increase the likelihood of having sexual encounters. As one user said of the effects of speed: "I feel more chatty, more able to talk and be assertive, so I don't feel so shy and insecure and vulnerable, which all makes for getting one's clothes off much easier... makes it easier to get them into bed."

Once in bed, stimulants were seen to 'speed up' the sexual encounter by 'shedding inhibitions', particularly when 'going to bed with someone for the first time'. This is because "you're not as embarrassed to do things" or to ask "for things you wouldn't ask people for unless you've known them for longer".

Do drugs encourage a loss of control?

Both alcohol and stimulants were seen to have disinhibitive effects, but alcohol was also seen to encourage sexual behaviours in which people said they had not wanted to engage. As was explained: "I've been really drunk and I've woken up the next day and thought 'Why the friggin' hell have I done this?'" As another said, with alcohol, "you can just really not know what you're doing."

In contrast, stimulants were not seen to encourage behaviours in which people did not want to engage. As one woman said about speed: "I don't think it makes you do anything that you don't want to do, your mind doesn't bend completely out of shape". Another said of cocaine: "I've never experienced losing my inhibitions to the point where I go home with somebody that I probably wouldn't have chosen to have gone home with". Whereas with stimulants your "brain's not affected" and you "definitely know what you're doing", with alcohol "anything can happen".

The disinhibitive effects of alcohol and stimulants were thus seen to manifest themselves differently in sexual encounters. Both substances were seen to help people lose their inhibitions, but alcohol was also seen to encourage a loss of control.

Does alcohol encourage unsafe sex?

A crucial question is whether the disinhibitive effects and loss of control associated with alcohol lead to unsafe sexual encounters. A typical response when asked why condoms were not used was: "Because I was very drunk. And it just happened". As the following example shows: "No, no, we didn't [use condoms]. We just sort of did it. That was it. Mind you, the thing was it was a deadly crime being a little drunk."

Others commented that alcohol encouraged unprotected sex despite prior intentions to use condoms: "When I drink alcohol I do things I wouldn't do if I were not on alcohol... for example, having sex without contraception, which is something I normally would never do."

But sexual safety is more than a question of whether or not condoms are used (Rhodes and Quirk, 1995a). Our study also showed that people perceived the effects of alcohol as encouraging a loss of control over the direction of sexual encounters. One interviewee, for example, described a situation where alcohol had "curbed all [his] inhibitions" to the point of having no control: "I let him tie me up into the most ridiculous position... He would have been able to do whatever he wanted to me... [which] as far as I'm concerned is the most foolish thing that one could ever do."

Alcohol was seen to encourage unsafe sex because it interfered with people's 'mental faculties' and adherence to 'reason'. This raises the question of whether alcohol or drunkenness can provide individuals with a justification or excuse for engaging in what are seen, by themselves or others, as unacceptable or 'bad' behaviours.

Do stimulants encourage unsafe sex?

Stimulants were not seen, in general, to encourage unsafe sex or a loss of control in sexual encounters. However, when people were asked to account for their own unsafe sexual behaviour, the effects of stimulants were nonetheless put forward as a reason. As users commented: "I've had unsafe sex because I've been off my head on acid or ecstasy", "I've allowed myself to have unsafe sex because of drugs" and "When taking drugs like speed, condoms are sometimes the last thing on your mind".

Users' accounts for why they themselves did not use condoms emphasised that stimulants do encourage a loss of control over "thinking" and decision-making where the pursuance of "pleasure" may take precedence over "reason". As one stimulant user commented: "It was because the drug was making me so knocked out in my brain that I didn't think about them [condoms]". As another explained: "You just lose control of yourself... your brain gets really tired and you can't think any more and all you think about is what's happening at that moment".

The key point to note here is the presence of contradictions both within as well as across interviewees' accounts. On the one hand, there is a consensus of opinion that stimulants do not encourage a loss of control over condom use. On the other hand, the effects of stimulants were put forward by users as reasons why they themselves had unsafe sex. These contradictions once again raise the question of whether drugs provide people with a justification or excuse for having had unsafe sex. It may be easier, for example, for me to say to a drugs worker or researcher that stimulants 'caused' me to have unsafe sex than it is for me to admit to wanting unsafe sex for other less easily justifiable reasons.

Drugs as 'reason' and 'excuse' for unsafe sex

Many surveys associate the use of alcohol and other drugs with an increased likelihood of having unsafe sex. But, in addition, they shed some light on why it is so difficult to establish what these associations actually mean. If alcohol or drugs provide a justification for 'bad behaviour' this introduces problems when determining whether or not alcohol or drugs actually cause unsafe sex. In client assessments, for example, it may be easier for people to say that alcohol encouraged them to have unsafe sex than to say that they had unsafe sex because they wanted to. It is questionable whether drug workers, researchers or people in general will be able to distinguish between 'reasons' and 'excuses' for unsafe sex (Rhodes and Quirk, 1995b).

This is not to suggest that people are necessarily, or consciously, lying about why they had unsafe sex. Rather, it highlights the social and cultural acceptability of using alcohol or drugs as an excuse and therefore says more about cultural 'norms' than it does about individuals' own explanations. This leads us to make two points about the role of future safe sex interventions.

First, interventions might aim to encourage a change in the view that alcohol or other drugs provide a socially acceptable excuse for unsafe sex. The aim would be to encourage an awareness that such an excuse is not acceptable. However, this approach may be limited, as the 'excuse potential' of drugs, and particularly of alcohol, is entrenched in everyday commonsense thinking (MacAndrew and Edgerton, 1969). It is something we all know about, and which many of us exploit in our day-to-day lives. What would be needed is a major upheaval in social and cultural norms and expectations about the effects of drugs. It would require, for example, changes in popular beliefs about the 'disinhibitive' effects of drugs and the extent to which individuals can make 'rational' choices after they have consumed drugs. In short, the aim would be to change our culture rather than individual drug and alcohol users. But such change cannot be brought about over night. This leads us to consider an alternative intervention approach.

Second, given that people currently associate drink and drug use with unsafe sex, it may be that the best intervention approach is to continue encouraging people to drink less and use fewer drugs prior to, and during, sexual encounters (Stall and Leigh, 1994). This is the case if we assume that drugs cause people to have unsafe sex against their better judgement (drugs as a 'reason'). It is also the case if we assume that people use and rationalise their drug use in ways which allow them to have unsafe sex (drugs as an 'excuse'). For those whose unsafe sex occurs on occasions where they have been drinking or using drugs, it might be best for interventions to emphasise safer levels of drinking and drug use. Unfortunate though it might be, interventions might even suggest that it is safer not to mix sex with drugs. If people are saying they lose control of themselves to the point that they 'forget' to use condoms, then interventions might remind people to think twice about drink or drugs and unprotected sex, in much the same way as people are reminded not to drink and drive.

References

MacAndrew C and Edgerton R B (1969) *Drunken Comportment: A Social Explanation*. Chicago: Aldine

Rhodes T and Quirk A (1995a) Sexual safety and drug use. *Executive Summary* 39, London: CRDHB

Rhodes T and Quirk A (1995b) Drugs as reason and excuse for mad, bad and unsafe behaviour. *Sixth international conference on the reduction of drug related harm*, Florence.

Stall R and Leigh B (1994) Understanding the relationship between drug or alcohol use and high-risk sexual activity for HIV transmission: where do we go from here? *Addiction*, 89: 131-134

This is an edited version of Executive Summary 40, April 1995, CRDHB, prepared by Tim Rhodes and Alan Quirk. It is reproduced with kind permission. A full version may be obtained from CRDHB, 200 Seagrove Road, London SW6 1RQ. 0181 846 6565, (free for those within the N. Thames area, otherwise £2.50. Cheques payable to the Charing Cross & Westminster Medical School.)

THE SCOTTISH DRUGS SCENE - AN OVERVIEW
Richard Hammersley, Behavioural Sciences Group
University of Glasgow

Is there a distinctly 'Scottish' drugs scene?

To begin with, some background information about Scotland: Scotland is just under two-thirds the size of England, but only contains about 3.5 million people. It has one large city, Glasgow (650,000), the smaller capital city, Edinburgh, and medium sized cities such as Dundee and Aberdeen. Most people in Scotland live in a central belt which includes Edinburgh, Glasgow, the 40 miles in between and surrounding towns. The Borders, Highlands and Islands have low population densities. Although most of the surface area of Scotland fits somewhat the kilts, castles, heather and haggis image purveyed by tourist boards, when we talk of the Scottish population we are talking mainly of a population who are either urban, or who live in towns which formerly depended for their livelihoods on heavy industries such as coal, steel and shipbuilding. Most people in Scotland live somewhere that is more like the North East of England than the Road to the Isles.

Social conditions tend to be somewhat harsher than in the South of England, and as bad, or worse, than the North. For example, there are long-standing high rates of unemployment, many areas of substandard housing, high rates of alcohol problems, smoking and of the diseases which result. On the other hand, the quality of life in Scotland tends to be higher than in England, in terms of affordable housing, lack of traffic, the ratio of amenities to population and access to the countryside. The high quality of life is probably mainly due to the relatively low population density. Perhaps it is also boosted by a fairly strong sense of national identity, which has increased over the last twenty years due to differences between the Conservative government in Westminster and the traditionally left politics of Scotland, particularly around Glasgow in the west.

Relatively few black people live in Scotland and most are ethnically from India and Pakistan, not being associated particularly with drug use more than anyone else. They might, given the potential links with drug producing countries, be associated with drug trafficking, but there is no evidence that this is the case. Traditional drug-taking practices, including cannabis and opium use, have not been imported to any great extent and drug use among young black Scots is similar, if sometimes more restrained and secretive, than among white Scots.

On the subject of trafficking, Scotland's large and sometimes fjord-like coastline is conducive to smuggling by boat. It is possible that some of the drugs sold throughout the UK land in Scotland. Again, evidence is patchy. There have been some very large seizures of drugs in recent years, but so have there been in England.

The Scottish legal system is different from the one in England and Wales. The key differences for understanding the drug scene are that (1) Scotland uses the law a lot. Per capita, Scotland imprisons more people than anywhere else in the EEC. About one third of men will reach 30 with a criminal record. (2) There are no probation officers in Scotland. (3) The relationship between the police and the prosecution is different. In Scotland the Procurator Fiscal receives information from the police and decides on prosecution. In short, when someone enters the legal system in Scotland, there is perhaps more momentum towards proceeding with the offence in a serious manner.

As elsewhere, Scottish police forces sometimes develop enthusiasms for tackling drug problems. In Strathclyde (which includes Glasgow) "Operation Eagle" combined aggressive policing of dealers with an educational campaign run by police officers. Many have questioned the appropriateness and suitability of the police adopting an educational role. Such criticism of Operation Eagle was rebutted on the basis that it at least showed that something could be done to combat the drug problem. This line of thinking has perhaps been continued in the all-party endorsed "Scotland Against Drugs" campaign funded, perhaps modestly, by a million pounds from Scottish Office coffers. This campaign has at least avoided the gross scare-mongering of earlier campaigns. In place of images of wasted or dead drug users we have the St Andrews flag with knotted ropes across it, which reminds me of the Boy Scouts more than anything else; perhaps intentionally. 'SAD' also features a touring bus decked out with this logo and was launched with TV publicity of leading Scottish politicians in SAD t-shirts and baseball caps dancing to modern dance music. The idea is to foster demiotic, local projects and have everyone pitch in against drugs, changing society's attitudes to them, as attitudes changed to drunk driving. Laudable, but perhaps not feasible.

The 1993 Scottish Crime Survey obtained the same data on self-reported drug use as the 1992 British Crime Survey (England & Wales). The figures were very similar and in both surveys, drug use was not restricted to urban or deprived areas and occurred at high levels among young people. Heroin use and cocaine use are rare ($<$ 1% and $<$2% respectively) at the population level. Information from agencies suggests that cocaine problems are rare in Scotland, compared to some cities in England including London and Birmingham.

Heroin problems are, however, just as common and Scottish heroin users are more likely to inject than their English counterparts. In consequence, the mid-80s saw considerable concern over and action on HIV prevention. At that time injectors had very high rates of infection in Edinburgh and low rates in Glasgow. Since, rates have dropped in Edinburgh and remain low elsewhere (drug injecting having spread to places like Dundee, Dumfries and Aberdeen in the meantime). The 1990s has seen an internationally unprecedented increase in drug overdose deaths in Glasgow. The reasons for this are still being investigated but injection of the benzodiazepine temazepam along with heroin may be one factor. Another drug that is less common further south is buprenorphine (temgesic) which is a synthetic painkiller. However, its misuse does not appear to cause any special problems, other than those already associated with drug injecting.

Cannabis use is widespread, but no more than in England. Use of stimulants and hallucinogens is also widespread and linked with the dance scene, as in England. Psilocybin mushrooms grow wild in abundance in Scotland and are commonly consumed during mushroom season.

Prevention in Scotland is confronted by the centrality of substance use and intoxication in Scottish culture. Simplified to the point of crudity: Scottish social life tends to consist of getting intoxicated and dancing or listening to music, usually at the same time. This applies as well to ceilidhs as to raves. Another problematic issue is the role of sharing substances in forming and maintaining social relationships. Many addiction researchers feel that the continued policy separation of drugs from alcohol and tobacco is unhelpful.

In summary, there are more similarities than differences between Scotland and England & Wales, particularly with the North of England. Key differences include the lack of a racial dimension to the problem, the absence of cocaine as a major issue and the high rates of injecting and overdose, with temazepam as a specific problem.

Is there a distinctly 'Scottish' solution?

The relatively left-wing, or at least liberal, traditions of Scotland mean that social justice is still seen as a valid orientation to social problems and social engineering approaches to social problems are perhaps more popular, or anyway more approved, than in the South of England. Debate about drug problems continues, but social consensus seems to be that drug use is a widespread fashion among young people which is reprehensible mainly because (i) there are acute dangers, including death and accidents and (ii) there is some risk of users moving on to dependence. It is also widely accepted that drug problems are largely the problems of drug injecting, which is associated with poverty and deprivation. The idea that reducing poverty and deprivation might reduce drug injecting is perhaps more acceptable as a basis for policy in Scotland than in the South of England. None of the following issues are unique to Scotland, but all are well-developed there.

Needle exchanges

Prior to HIV, the treatment response to drugs in Scotland was a varied array of often ill-funded agencies offering many different treatment services with little integration. The first systematic step after HIV was the addition of needle exchanges, despite initial public concerns. In Glasgow the first needle exchange was picketed for six months. Concerns about increased neighbourhood problems were not realised and eventually some areas requested exchanges of their own, rather than opposing them. The Glasgow exchanges take in more syringes than they distribute and serve as an important method of getting and keeping injectors in contact with services. They also revealed many injectors whose problems were less extreme than those who had previously attended treatment. Thanks in part to these exchanges, less than 2% of drug injectors in Glasgow are HIV positive.

Methadone

In the mid- 1980s, there was considerable unease and confusion about prescribing to drug users. Many GPs and psychiatrists were reluctant to prescribe at all. Others prescribed drugs including codeine products, benzodiazepines and temgesic, which may not be that helpful. After concerns about HIV a drug prescribing service was set up in Edinburgh, headed by Judy Greenwood. This service encouraged GPs to prescribe methadone and provided them with the training and support to do so. A similar service was set up in Glasgow in 1994. Both have been very successful and Edinburgh appears to have experienced reductions in drug related harm, as well as crime during the time the service has been in operation. There is still some opposition to methadone among those who favour abstinence-based approaches, but methadone's practical benefits have won over most people, despite ethical concerns about prescribing to, even sedating, drug users.

Most medical treatment of drug users now occurs in this context, with users coming off methadone when they are ready to do so, rather than moving around a turntable of treatment based abstinence and community relapse.

Widespread dialogue between all concerned parties

Over the last decade, there has been more open discussion of drug problems, involving a wider spectrum of views. Drug users themselves have become involved in this discussion in three ways. First, ex-user groups, most famously Calton Athletic which combines mutual support, abstinence and sport, have become skilful at presenting their views in the media. Second, the dance scene has developed its own drug advisers, such as Crew 2000, and its own media (M8 magazine). Their view of drugs is about tolerance and caution rather than total abstinence. Third, the Scottish Prison Service has developed a drugs policy based in part on conferences including inmates as delegates. Several prisons have introduced mixtures of treatment in prison and a balanced approach to the issue of drugs in prison, including the use of drug-free areas of prison maintained by voluntary drug screening. The impact of mandatory drug testing on these initiatives remains to be seen.

Scapegoating of drugs for social problems

Nonetheless, as elsewhere, drug users, particularly injectors, are still sometimes used as the focus for explaining the problems of poverty and deprivation. Never mind inadequate housing and amenities, little education and few work prospects, things for youth would somehow be magically better if they avoided drugs. However, because injecting is so widespread among young people in some areas, there is now less demonisation of injectors in general and public attitudes are moving beyond a simple black and white view of the drugs problem.

Normalisation of some drug use among the young

At the same time, as elsewhere in Britain, drug use has become very widespread in Scotland among people under 30. Some surveys suggest that more than half have at least tried drugs and over 20% have taken them more than a few times. Most drug users still smoke cannabis more than anything else, but they are also likely to have taken other substances, including amphetamines, hallucinogens and ecstasy. A smaller number will also try cocaine and opiates. Despite widespread drug use, which may represent a huge increase (we do not have comparable earlier figures), rates of heroin and cocaine dependence do not seem to be increasing.

Urban renewal

There have been concerted efforts to revive some of the most deprived areas of Scottish cities. In Glasgow, some of the worst housing stock of low and high-rise flats has been renovated and new attempts have been made to introduce amenities, even work, into the worst areas. It remains to be seen whether these efforts will be successful in the long term. Although not directed against drugs in particular, some renovated flats now have a concierge system and CCTV which at least discourages the stairs from being used as shooting galleries.

A lot of drugs researchers

Glasgow alone contains more drugs researchers than anywhere else outside London. We are somewhat ill-organised and quarrelsome, which perhaps fits Southern stereotypes of Glaswegians, although many of us are originally English. There is also drugs research in Edinburgh and Stirling. One very substantial project is the MRC WHO study of drug injectors, for which Glasgow is one of several international sites. This has gathered more quantitative information about drug injecting that was previously available.

The 'Glasgow School' of drugs research
Drugs research in Glasgow occurs at all four Universities (Glasgow, Glasgow Caledonian, Strathclyde and Paisley) as well at in the various Health Boards. There is no formal structure to this work, but certain common themes are apparent to me. It

- emphasises psycho-social factors and includes sociologists, psychologists, anthropologists and health professionals. The MRC WHO study is one example of this approach.
- treats drug use as a personal choice, if often a flawed one. John B. Davies' work on attribution and addiction is a clear example.
- generates non-pathological accounts of drug using behaviours. Neil McKeganey & Marina Barnard, as well as Avril Taylor, have examined the world of the heroin injector from this kind of perspective.
- places drug problems in the context of alcohol and tobacco. Work on adolescents by Niall Coggans, Marion Henderson, Neil McKeganey & Marina Barnard, myself with Tara Lavelle & Alasdair Forsyth has examined the spectrum of substance use.
- examines people outwith clinics. Samples have been obtained on the street, by snowballing, or from agencies such as needle exchanges which have a wider net than 'addicts with problems". Jason Ditton and colleagues have examined cocaine users and more recently ecstasy users in this manner. David Shewan & Phil Delgano are currently studying recreational heroin users.

It is difficult to assess the impact that this research activity has on the Scottish drugs scene. We get quite a lot of media coverage which, boiled down to the bare minimum, consists of many of us saying "Its not that simple, or that bad" over and over again. In the meantime, perhaps the response to drugs has moved beyond simplistic attempts to stamp them out for the greater good.

Suggested reading
Davies, J.B. (1992) *The myth of addiction*. Reading: Harwood.

Ditton, J. & Hammersley, R. H. (1996) *A very greedy drug: Cocaine in context*. Reading: Harwood.

Frischer, M., Bloor, M., Goldberg, D., Clark, J., Green, S. & Mckeganey, N. (1993) Mortality among injecting drug users: a critical reappraisal. *Journal of Epidemiology and Community Health, 47*, 59-63.

Hammersley, R. H. (1994) *Drug misuse in Scotland: Data from the Scottish Crime Survey*. Edinburgh: HMSO.

Hammersley, R. H., Cassidy, M.T. & Oliver, J. (1995) Drugs associated with drug related deaths in Edinburgh and Glasgow November 1990 to October 1992. *Addiction*, 90, 959-965.

Hammersley, R. H. & Pearl, S. (1996) Drug use and other problems of residents in projects for the young, single homeless. *Health and Social Care in the Community*, 4, 193-199.

Kahn, F., Ditton, J., Hammersley, R. H. & Short, E. (1996) *Drug using attitudes* and *behaviour of young members of ethnic minority groups in Glasgow*. Drug Prevention Initiative Report. Forthcoming

McKegancy, N. P. & Barnard, M. (1992) *AIDS, drugs and sexual risk: lives in the balance*. Buckingham: Open University Press.

Robertson, J. R. (1987) *Heroin, AIDS and society*. London: Hodder and Stoughton.

Taylor, A., Frischer, M., Green, S., Goldberg, E., Mckeganey, N. & Gruer, L. (1994) Low and stable prevalence of HIV among drug injectors in Glasgow. *International Journal of Sexually Transmitted Diseases and AIDS, 5*, 105-107.

Taylor, Avril (1993) *Women drug users: an ethnography of a female injecting community*. Oxford: Clarendon Press.

My earlier work on the drugs-crime connection may also be of interest
Hammersley, R. H., Forsyth, A.J.M & Lavelle, T.L. (1990) The criminality of new drug users in Glasgow. *British Journal of Addiction*, 85, 1583-1594.

Hammersley, R. H., Forsyth, A.J.M, Morrison, V.L. & Davies, J.B. (1989) The relationship between crime and opioid use. *British Journal of Addiction, 84*, 1029-1043.

DRUGS POLICY IN THE NETHERLANDS
FACTS AND FIGURES: CONTINUITY AND CHANGE
Dr. Irene Sagel-Grande, State University of Leiden, The Netherlands

1.   Preface

The laws and legal regulations of any particular country need to be seen in the context of the national legal culture of which they are a part, if they are to be understood and judged correctly. There is a good deal of misunderstanding in other countries about Dutch drugs policy, mainly because people are apt to look at it and judge it on the basis of their own legal culture and not in the context of the Dutch legal culture and policies. In what follows I will try to resolve some of the misunderstanding by presenting the Dutch drugs policy in its true context.

First I should like to point out that the Netherlands have signed the Treaty of Geneva of 1925, the Single Convention on Narcotic Drugs of 1961, the Single Convention of 1976, the Convention of Vienna of 1988, the Convention of Strasbourg of 1990 and finally also the Convention on Psychotropic Substances of 1971.

2.   The Dutch Narcotics Act

The Dutch Narcotics Act dates from 1928, but was amended fundamentally in 1976. Since then there have been further minor amendments, but no substantial changes. This is a clear indication that the Dutch legislators consider that the law passed in 1976 is a good basis on which to fight drug crime in the Netherlands.

What was decided in 1976?

•   Differentiation between the different substances

The most important decision made was to make a clear distinction between so-called hard and soft drugs. List 1 contained the hard drugs and list 2 the soft drugs. At that time, only cannabis products were considered soft drugs and list 1 contained all substances except cannabis. Thus a very clear distinction was made, based on the idea that cannabis was less dangerous than all other drugs as it seemed to be almost non-addictive, or at least not physically addictive. Since then, new research results have appeared which indicate that regular smoking of large quantities of hashish has a definite negative influence on learning ability and memory[1], so there seem to be more risks with using cannabis then were apparent in 1976. However the 1976 regulation had the advantage of clarity; everybody could understand it and consequently it had an influential effect on public opinion.

The division between cannabis and the substances of list 1 was made mainly in the hope of avoiding progression from soft drugs to hard drugs. The idea was, and is, to try to separate the hard drug market from the soft drug market, and the hard drug dealers from the soft drug dealers.

•   Differentiation between major and minor offences

Dutch penal law divides criminality into major and minor offences. Almost all offences in the Narcotics Act are major offences, but possession of soft drugs for own use is a minor offence (but still a criminal offence).

•   Differentiation between roles in the drug scene

The Dutch Narcotics Act differentiates between offenders in various ways, firstly and most importantly, between dealers and consumers, secondly between hard drug dealers and soft drug dealers and thirdly between international and national dealers.

•   The main criminal offences and their ranges of punishment under the Dutch Narcotics Act

Figures 1 and 2 set out the offences and the sentencing system created by the Act.

Figure 1: Hard drugs offences and their punishments under the Dutch Narcotics Act

Offences	I. Import/export not for own use (intentionally)	II. Making, working up etc. not for own use (intentionally)	III. Keeping in stock not for own use (intentionally)	IV. As I-III but not intentionally	V. As I and III but small quantities for own use (intentionally)
Max sentences	12 years or 100,000 Guilders	8 years or 100,000 Guilders	4 years or 100,000 Guilders	6 months or 25,000 Guilders	1 year or 10,000 Guilders

Figure 2: Soft drugs offences and their punishments under the Dutch Narcotics Act

Offences	1. Import/Export not for own use (intentionally)	11. Making, working up, keeping in stock etc. not for own use (intentionally)	III. As I and 11 but small quantities for own use (intentionally or not intentionally)
Max sentences	4 years or 100,000 Guilders	2 years or 25,000 Guilders	max. 1 month or 5,000 Guilders

In the Netherlands the import and export, dealing in, preparing, keeping in stock, possession, etc, of both hard and soft drugs are criminal offences, in accordance with the international conventions that we signed. Actually, the Dutch Narcotics Act does not cover the use of drugs, so drug use itself is not an offence. But how do you use drugs without possessing them? We must conclude that the Dutch legislation does not make the Netherlands the narcotic paradise many people seem to think.

3. Distinguishing features of the Dutch drugs policy

The principles on which the Dutch Narcotics Act is based are the same as those of Dutch criminal law policy in general, ie sobriety, pragmatism, search for the happy medium, humanity and tolerance of the freely chosen life-style of others.

The Dutch give higher priority to the public health problems posed by drugs than to the penal law problems. Education, prevention, medical and other kinds of help are therefore given more importance in the Netherlands than prosecution and sentencing. This is exemplified by the fact that the substitute drug methadone has been given to hard drug addicts, including those in the prisons, for the last twenty years (at present about 7,000 addicts receive daily methadone in the Netherlands). That does not mean that the penal law is not used in the fight against drugs. Long prison sentences are given, mainly in cases of international organised trade, and this is the main reason for the rapid growth in the prison population in the Netherlands in recent years.

4. Dutch legal practice until 1996
• The principle of discretionary prosecution

It is generally known that law in the books and law in practice are not the same. Dutch legal practice includes discretionary prosecution, determined by the public prosecutor. Prosecution can be waived on grounds of the public good. An appeal can be made against this to a higher level of the department of public prosecution or to the Minister of Justice.

This principle of discretionary prosecution is deeply rooted in Dutch legal culture and tradition. Old Dutch law included ways of settling a penal case out of court, known as the submission and the composition. In modern times, the possibility of a "transaction", that is an agreed fine imposed by the prosecutor, has been introduced. Out of court settlement is possible in all cases where an offence is punishable with no higher sentence than 6 years imprisonment or a fine.

According to Art 74, sub 2, Dutch Penal Code the prosecutor can impose the following conditions:

- Payment of an amount of at least 5 Guilders and not exceeding the maximum fine stipulated in the statutory definition relating to the matter in question.
- Renunciation of seized objects which are subject to confiscation (penalty) or to withdrawal (measure).
- Renunciation of objects which are subject to confiscation or payment of their estimated value to the state.
- Payment of an amount to the state equivalent to the estimated benefit gained through or in connection with the offence.
- Total or partial compensation for the damage caused by the punishable act.

The prosecutor can choose one or more of these conditions, or can use alternative sanctions. Prosecution can be waived either under a condition or unconditionally.

There are three main explanations for the extent of the use of transactions and conditional waiver of prosecution in recent years:

1) The rise in crime and the growing influence of international organised crime. Discretionary prosecution allows concentration on the most dangerous forms of crime.
2) The Dutch judiciary and police are both relatively small organizations compared with those in other countries, nevertheless the costs of the administration of justice are high. Devolving part of the responsibility of the judiciary to the Department of Public Prosecution improves effectiveness in the fight against crime. One of the most important reasons however is very simple and pragmatic - the costs of one court sentence are about the same as for five prosecution transactions.
3) Discretionary prosecution provides an important means of deciding cases that are controversial because majority public opinion no longer supports the law. The Department of Public Prosecution has often prevented the escalation of dissatisfaction in society by deciding not to prosecute people for certain controversial offences, such as squatting, offences against public order (handing raisins to people on the street during the hippy and provo periods), abortion, euthanasia and also possessing small quantities of soft drugs.

Because of the extension of the transaction power of the Department of Public Prosecution, what used to be the normal criminal procedure has become more and more the exception. Nowadays about 50% of all criminal cases are settled out of court by transactions or conditional or unconditional waiver. The five senior Public Prosecutors and the courts of appeal who, together with a high official of the Ministry of Justice, meet regularly to discuss guidelines based on the latest criminal justice policy, decided recently[2] that in 1998 about 30% of major charges should be settled by prosecutor transactions, ie without bringing the case before a judge. In the longer term, they plan to settle about 50% of major cases in this way.

The Minister of Justice is responsible to parliament for the guidelines.

- **The Guidelines to the Narcotics Act 1976**

The guidelines regularly advise public prosecutors how to apply the Narcotics Act in accordance with the latest drugs policy. It also clarifies the meaning of the term "for own use", as used in the Narcotics Act. "For own use" is considered to mean "a small quantity to be used in a day". For hard drugs, the present version of the guideline suggests that is one LSD-trip, $1/2$g of amphetamine, heroin, morphine or cocaine or 30g of cannabis. The public prosecutor is not bound by the guidelines if there are important reasons for a different decision.

Figures 3 and 4 show the guideline suggested sentences, varying according to the important principle of differentiation between hard and soft drugs, in order to realise the aims of the drugs policy. The maximum sentences recommended in the guidelines are much lower than the law allows, but this is in line with the usual difference between legal maxima and the lengths of sentences that are passed in practice.

The recommended sentences mirror the policy of giving priority to fighting hard drugs over soft drugs, and the wish for relatively hard penalties to be imposed on traders and dealers, while users are seen mainly as people who need help rather than sanctions. Sentences for users are mild, and in cases of soft drugs the charges can even be waived. This has a considerable bearing on investigation.

Figure 3: Guideline '76: Hard Drugs

Offences	I. Import/export not for own use (intentionally)	II. Making, working up etc. not for own use (intentionally)	III. Keeping in stock not for own use (intentionally)	IV. As 1-111 not intentionally	V. As I and II for own use
max. sentence Narcotics Act	12 years or 100,000 Guilders	8 years or 100,000 Guilders	4 years or 100,000 Guilders	6 months or 25,000 Guilders	1 year or 10,000 Guilders
Participation as	dealer courier	dealer courier	dealercourier		
Guideline '76	< 3 yrs > 2 yrs	> 2 yrs (part I.) cond. prison sentence possible	> 1 (part I.) year cond. prison sentence		conditional dismissal

Figure 4: Guideline '76: Soft Drugs

Offences	I. Import/export not for own use (intentionally)	II. Keeping in stock, making not for own use (intentionally)	As I and II but small quantities (3og for cannabis) for own use intentionally or as I and II but not intentionally
Max. sentence Narcotics Act	4 years or 100,000 Guilders	2 years or 25,000 Guilders	1 month or 5,000 Guilders
Guideline '76	> 1 year	unconditional prison sentence or fine	transaction or dismissal (waiver)

- **Investigation, Prosecution and Sentencing**

Dealing in and possession of, etc, all kinds of drugs are punishable offences under the Narcotics Act, and investigation as well as prosecution mainly follows the guidelines. Figure 5 shows that the Netherlands do not lag behind other European countries in the seizure of drugs by customs, the police and other investigation agencies:

Since 1986 there has been a rapid rise in long prison sentences (longer than 4 years) in the Netherlands. They had doubled by 1991 and have continued to rise. This is mainly due to the extent of the drugs crime and the prison sentences are being used to fight it.

The Narcotics Act guidelines were evaluated in 1988[4] and it was found that the public prosecutors were following the guidelines on the waiver of cases quite strictly, but were going further than the guideline recommends in differentiation between cases. The weight of the drugs involved was being used as a criterion in hard drug cases, and in cases of possession of not more than 3g of hard drugs the charge was waived. That means that the weight differentials used in practice are higher than those given in the guidelines. The research also found that the public prosecutors almost always keep below the maximum sentences recommended in the guidelines.

Figure 6 shows how discretionary prosecution operates in relation to Narcotics Act offences.

There are about 1,500 - 1,700 coffee shops which sell drugs in the Netherlands at present, about 350 of them in Amsterdam. Cannabis products are also sold in pubs, by house dealers, etc. An attempt has been made recently to reduce the number of coffee shops in several cities and to keep them under tighter control. The reason is that people living in the neighbourhood of coffee shops have often been disturbed by their customers.

Figure 5: Comparative overview of seizures of illegal drugs[3]

1994	NL	FR	GER	B	SP
Heroin (kg)	246	661	1.590	137	824
Cocaine (kg)	8,200	4,743	767	479	3,899
Cannabis (kg)	238,258	58,014	25,694	59,904	219,195
Amphetamine (kg)	215	80	120	23	32
Synthetic drugs/ tablets (x 1000)	143	329	30	61	314

Figure 6

Difference between hard and soft drug offences		
hard drugs, 5,737		soft drugs, 1,579
50.7%	waived	42.9%
5.9%	combined	1.5%
3.1%	transaction	37.8%
38.1%	sentenced	15.7%
1.7%	not guilty	1.1%

• **Drug-selling coffee shops**

The sale of drugs in Dutch coffee shops follows from the different attitude to hard drugs and cannabis products. Although it is against the law, selling and buying cannabis is tolerated by the practice of discretionary prosecution provided five criteria are fulfilled. The five criteria were laid down in a special coffee-shop guideline in 1991. They are:

(1) Not more than 30g to be sold (per person)
(2) No dealing in hard drugs
(3) No advertising or advertising signs
(4) No disturbance of the public order
(5) No selling to minors.

The use of discretionary prosecution by the Department of Public Prosecution to tolerate the existence of coffee shops is not just a question of the most effective use of scarce resources in the fight against crime, but also depends upon the broad public tolerance of soft drug users in Dutch society. If it were for not the International Conventions which they have signed, the Netherlands would certainly prefer to legalise the use of small quantities, and even dealing in small quantities in coffee shops, under a state monopoly or a licensing system. The Dutch Labour Party, which supports proposals for this limited legalisation, declares that this would be the best way to reduce the involvement of organised crime in coffee shops. General decriminalisation finds less public support, as it would mean increased risks, mainly for public health and for traffic safety. Most people in the Netherlands are aware that the 1990 Convention is an obstacle to any legalisation of cannabis products.

• **Nedweed**

The result of practising discretionary prosecution for the use of soft drugs is that a new illegal economic activity has developed, the production of cannabis. The quantity of cannabis that is produced in the Netherlands is not known for certain, but according to research it must be about 40 tons a year, and of high quality (up to 40% THC!). Nedweed already covers 50% of the Dutch soft drugs market, and new problems are now arising for the Dutch government as it appears that more and more Nedweed is being exported.

• Hard Drug Addicts and Criminality

It is difficult to say to what extent the aim of the strict differentiation between hard drugs and soft drugs in the Dutch Narcotics Act has been met, ie to keep the markets separated and to avoid soft drug users starting to use hard drugs. On the other hand we can state that the practice in the Netherlands, ie discretionary prosecution based on differentiation, has not resulted in the appearance of more hard drug addicts than there are in most other countries, as can be seen in figure 7.

Figure 7: International comparative prevalence figures on hard drug addicts

	Total no of addicts	No per 1000 of population
Netherlands	25,000	1.6
Germany	100,000/120,000	1.3/1.5
Belgium	17,500	1.8
Luxembourg	2,000	5.0
France	135,000/150,000	2.4/2.6
United Kingdom	150,000	2.6
Denmark	10,000	2.0
Sweden	13,500	1.6
Norway	4,500	1.0
Switzerland	26,500/45,000	4.0/6.7
Austria	10,000	1.3
Italy	175,000	3.0
Spain	120,000	3.0
Greece	35,000	3.5
Portugal	45,000	4.5
Ireland	2,000	0.6

Sources: Bosman and Van Es (1993); Bless, Korf, Freeman, Urban drug policies in Europe 1993 (1993); WHO regional office for Europe, European summary on drug abuse, first report: 1985-1990 (1992); Commission of the European Communities, Second Report on drug demand reduction in the European Community (1992); Bossong (1994), van Cauwenberghe at al. 1993 (Belgium).[5]

There has been a good deal of research on the connection between criminality and addiction[6]. In the Netherlands it has been established that about 50% of the addicts had committed offences before they became addicts. Crime committed by addicts therefore cannot be entirely explained as the consequence of addiction. It seems more likely that deviant behaviour and/or a deviant personality causes addiction as well as criminal behaviour. Further research[7] indicates that addicts' level of use depends strongly on how much money they have. Most addicts are poly-drug users. They often use heroin and cocaine in combination. An average quantity for a week costs about 500 Guilders for heroin and 750 Guilders for cocaine. The average user gains about 20% of his or her income from crime, 28% from social welfare benefits, 22% from prostitution and 18% from dealing. Among the population that was the subject of the research, "only" 37% were committing offences in order to get money for drugs. So addiction does not necessarily lead to crime.

Another interesting finding of the research was that giving addicts methadone had no effect on the amount of crime they committed.

Dutch practice in the area of narcotics, like our practice in relation to other offences, follows our own tradition and legal culture that have grown up in the course of a long evolution. The Netherlands have incorporated into our own law the international standards that are required by the many International Conventions on drugs to which we have signed up, but the practical application of the law is based on the general principles of the Dutch legal culture.

It can further be stated that the Dutch policy of tolerance of soft drug use has not resulted in an alarmingly high level of consumption among young people, and that users of soft drugs do not as a rule tend to experiment with hard drugs.

The policy on drug addicts concentrates mainly on prevention and care, with the result that the health of addicts in the Netherlands compares favourably with that in other countries. There is less widespread HIV infection among Dutch addicts, and their mortality rate is low, and not increasing as it is in many countries.

5. The Future of Drugs Policy in the Netherlands: Continuity and Change
In spring 1996 the Dutch drugs policy[8] was discussed in Parliament. It concluded that the policy has led to satisfactory results so far, and therefore there was no reason for much change. It was not proposed that either hard or soft drugs would be legalised. The strict differentiation between hard and soft drugs, and between users and dealers, etc, will continue, as will the integrated approach, ie prevention, care and social rehabilitation, with penalties under the criminal law for criminal behaviour and nuisance.

But a number of negative implications were recognised, such as,
1) intense nuisance caused by (hard) drug users to the general public,
2) the great attraction of the "Dutch Treat"[9] for foreign users, resulting in criticism abroad, and
3) the increasing involvement of criminal organisations in the supply and sale of drugs at home and abroad.

So as well as continuity there must be a certain change. A number of plans have been proposed to improve the situation, some of the most important of which are as follows:

- the revision of care for addicts (greater range of residential care to be provided, more attention to be paid to prevention and to addicts' social problems, trials involving the provision of heroin to older, untreatable addicts, increased capacity in compulsion and dissuasion projects (500 places in consultation with Public Prosecution Department), opening of a forensic addiction clinic with 70 places),
- the establishment of a panel of experts to assist municipalities in tackling the problem of nuisance, using administrative powers and pursuing an agreed policy on coffee shops,
- a strict approach to drug tourists who cause nuisance (immediate deportation),
- a Bill to create a criminal law power to allow addicts who frequently commit offences or cause nuisance to be taken into care compulsorily,
- the amount of cannabis whose retail sale is tolerated in regulated coffee-shops to be reduced from 30g to 5g,
- closer monitoring of drug exportation,
- a Bill to increase the maximum penalty for cultivation of cannabis,
- investigation of the large-scale cultivation of Nedweed as a matter of priority,
- promotion of cross-border cooperation,
- greater emphasis on the investigation of criminal organisations,
- increased research, monitoring and evaluation,
- more effort to be put into the development of new drugs.

6.   Conclusion
The Dutch Narcotics Act is, and will remain, compatible with international conventions. Its practical application follows the same traditions as all our other penal laws. The principle of discretionary prosecution, which is one of the most typical principles of the Dutch legal culture, gives the Narcotics Act its practical interpretation and sense. Each country has developed its own language, its own history, its own way of thinking, its own sense of humour and its own legal traditions. All these special characteristics, however, come together in collaboration in European or other international contexts. The Dutch drugs policy is a good example for this. If the rich diversity between nations is to be preserved, tolerance of phenomena such as the Dutch drugs policy will be essential.

1. PET (Positron-Emission-Tomography) Research done in the Brookhaven Laboratory in New York State by a team under the leadership of Joana Fowler.
2. NRC/HBI. of 10.6.1996
3. Policy Document: Drugs Policy in the Netherlands, Continuity and Change, 1995, p. 52.

4. Rook, J.J.A. Essers: Vervolging en Strafvordedng bij opiumdelicten 1988.
5. Policy Paper: Drugs Policy in the Netherlands, 1995, p. 9.
6. M. Grapendaal, Ed. Leuw, J.M. Nolen: De economic van het drugsbostaan, 1991.
7. M. Grapendaal: De markt van wit en bruin. De Psycholoog, 1989, p. 357-363.
8. Policy Paper, Drugs Policy in the Netherlands, Continuity and Change, 1995.
9. D.J. Korf, Dutch Treat, formal control and illicit drug use in the Netherlands, Amsterdam 1995.

——————— • ———————

DRUG PROBLEMS IN ESTONIA
Sirje Sepalaan, Chief Medical Officer,
the Estonian Correction and Executive Board

Estonia is a small country with a population of about 1.5 million people. It is the main route for drug-dealers from the East to the West. We didn't have any drug problems until the year 1995. There were 6.2 drug abusers per 100,000 in 1970, 6.2 in 1980 and 18 in 1990. 80% of them are users of illicit home-made products such as poppy capsules and opium. 95% of the users are men, 75% are non-Estonians and 70% are younger than 40. Most of the drug-users have a criminal background.

Alcohol is another problem in our country. Statistics show that 12-14 litres of pure alcohol are consumed per person per year. In 1994 there were 670 cases of alcohol intoxication in Estonian prisons, in 1995, 599 cases. The quantity of alcohol confiscated was 982.6 litres last year. Medical treatment of drug-abusers is voluntary. There are two big treatment centres, Wismari hospital in Tallinn and a private clinic in Tartu. We have also a psychiatrist in each district. Consultation is free for the members of National Health Service.

We don't have a Drugs Law yet, but one is being drafted at the Office of Justice, the Ministry of Health and the Ministry of Labour. In the criminal code we have 7 sections, connected with drugs. We also have a commission of 5 ministers in our government, who elaborate the state politics of drugs. The Estonian Parliament decided to join the narcotic convention of the United Nations Organisation.

Crimes committed under the influence of intoxication are increasing year after year. We had 15 drug-abusers in two remand prisons in May 1995. Today we have about 200 (among them 12 teenagers). In the prison we seldom see drug intoxication: in 1994 - 6 cases and in 1995 - 11 cases. Most of the drug-users, who are tested in the prison, are infected by Hepatitis B and C. In the central Prison Hospital we have had 8 cases of acute Hepatitis during the current year. Some cases were very serious. Ways are being worked out to reduce the usage of drugs in the prison:

1.   to organise better social, spiritual and psychological work
2.   to allow the sale of cigarettes only in the prison shop
3.   to ensure that medicine is taken in the presence of medical workers
4.   to enhance supervision.

THE DEVELOPMENT OF ILLEGAL DRUGS TRAFFIC IN ROMANIA, & THE WORK OF THE CUSTOMS AUTHORITIES
Michaela Dragos, Head of Anti-Narcotics Division
Romanian General Customs Administration

Up to 1990, the dangers of the illegal drugs traffic did not constitute a major problem for Romania. Although Romania has always been a transit country between the Middle East and Western Europe due to its geographical position, being a potential link on the Balkan route for heroin traffic, drug dealers seldom used the transit through our country because of the closed community system prevailing here up to 1990. The classical Balkan route for heroin today began in Turkey (a country of origin for drugs), went through Bulgaria and the former Yugoslavia as countries of transit reaching directly the user countries from Western Europe (Italy, Austria, Germany and Netherlands).

Political, economic and social changes throughout Eastern Europe at the end of 1989 enabling the opening of borders, the distorted image of democracy, the lack of suitable legislation, the lack of technical equipment and specialised institutions to prevent and fight illegal drugs traffic generated new opportunity for the international drugs dealers. The beginning of the war in the former Yugoslavia involved among other things, the changing of the drugs dealers' routes. Starting in 1990, the Balkan drugs traffic route was diverted, Romania becoming after a short time an important link. The present route for heroin from the Middle East to Western Europe passes through 80% of Romania.

The introduction of a market economy and the transition this involves inevitably engender negative as well as positive changes in the life of a people. This happened in Romania too, where the urge for a quick rise in the living standards of many people coupled with the lack of a suitable punishment legislation (the maximum penalty for illegal drugs trafficking is 7 years of imprisonment according to the present Customs Code and only 5 years according to the Criminal Law) has generated their involvement in drug trafficking.

As a result, Romania has moved from a transit country, to a warehousing country. This means that drugs entering the country in huge quantities are deposited with the help of national criminal organisations and are then exported using different smuggling methods often involving Romanian carriers.

Other factors which have encouraged illegal drugs trafficking in Romania are:

- The situation in the neighbouring countries: Poland has become a manufacturing country for chemical drugs in the laboratory - amphetamines and LSD; the growing of opium poppy and the production of native drugs known as 'Black Polish Soup' or 'Kompott' has spread over here too.
- The political, social and economic changes within the former Soviet Union have increased tourism towards Western Europe and with it the illegal drugs traffic risk. As is well-known in the Asian parts of the former Soviet Union cannabis was grown widely, thus marijuana, hashish, opium and heroin could be easily obtained and sent to Europe (including Romania).
- Constantza Harbour is the fifth largest port in Europe and it is an area of high risk for drugs imports mainly from African countries and Turkey. During 1993, customs officers from Constantza have discovered and seized a total of 10 tons of marijuana and hashish.
- The large number of Turkish, Arab and Chinese citizens resident in Romania, provide the opportunity, under the cover of import-export trade activities, to perform drug deals and the laundering of money obtained from those activities.
- The existence in Romania of a large number of emigrants from Nigeria, Pakistan, Afghanistan, Tanzania and Lebanon, provide an opportunity, through their efforts to get to Western Europe, for illegal drugs trafficking.
- Romania is attracting more and more networks of traffickers smuggling hashish from Africa and cocaine from South America towards Western Europe, mainly Germany, Netherlands, Spain, Italy, Belgium and Austria amongst others.
- The post-revolutionary youth are proving most vulnerable to the attractions of the illegal drugs traffic. Willing to make quick money, they agree to act as carriers for relatively small sums ($2000-$3000). Before 1994, the great majority of the people involved in drugs trafficking were foreigners. After 1994 the number of Romanian nationals involved in such activities increased markedly and is now more than 60%.
- Imports and transits of goods from South American countries, countries of high risk, cocaine producers and dealers.

Regarding drugs consumption in Romania, we can say that the inevitable has occurred; we have, unfortunately begun to have our own consumers, from among the youth, rockers and prostitutes. Attempts are being made to obtain new markets by selling at very low prices as compared to the international market and introducing drugs in schools, colleges, student hostels and discos.

Another facet of the illegal drugs traffic in Romania is the diversion of chemical substances and precursors which are used in clandestine laboratories to obtain synthetic drugs. In this respect, many foreign companies, mostly from Turkey, try to contact Romanian chemical works to acquire essential chemicals. In conclusion, we can state that Romania is now a country of transit, storage, export and consumption for the illegal drugs trade.

The work of the Customs Authorities

Through their activities in examining and checking documents, extending from travellers, to freight and conveyances, at the border as well as inside the country, the customs authorities have placed the first barrier in the way of the illegal drugs traffic. They are becoming an important state force in the prevention and fighting of this menace.

The Enforcement Department was organised within the General Customs Administration in 1993. Its operations include, among others, the Drugs Enforcement Division and the Drugs Testing Laboratory.

The work of the central Drugs Enforcement Office includes:
- the collection, analysis and transmission of internal and international information
- operational investigations and activities
- the synthesis, analysis and evaluation of the aspects and problems of illegal drugs trafficking, their adaptation to the peculiarities of our country and the taking of appropriate countermeasures
- the training of customs officers in this field
- co-operation with the officers of the Ministry of the Interior, of the Health Ministry, of the Culture Ministry and of other specialised institutions engaged in the activity of illegal drugs trafficking prevention and fighting
- assessment and location of the necessary technical equipment to deal with practical problems of customs units.

Special attention is given to training, by organising courses not only with Romanian experts, but also with experts from customs administrations belonging to countries displaying a wider experience in this field like the United Kingdom, Germany and the USA.

The Drugs Testing Laboratory, is equipped with modern analytical equipment, meeting international standards, according to the model of the Drugs Laboratory from the United Kingdom. When substances suspected of being narcotic drugs, precursors or psychotropic substances are found at the customs units, the samples taken are sent without delay to the drugs testing lab, where they are subjected to qualitative and quantitative analyses. Reports are issued containing exact data about the nature of the substance, so that the case can be turned over with a complete supporting documentation to the criminal investigation experts.

Programmes for co-operation, mutual assistance and bilateral and trilateral action have been established with the customs administrations from Bulgaria and Hungary. These activities include: an operational information exchange on suspect persons, vehicles, carriers and companies, on their modus operandi and on the new routes adopted for the illegal drugs trafficking; the organising and carrying out of joint bilateral and trilateral operations; and the organising of intensive and simultaneous actions in the most exposed border crossing units. There also exists a draft agreement between the Government of the Turkish Republic and the Government of Romania regarding illegal drugs traffic and the use of narcotic drugs and psychotropic substances.

Romania has ratified all UN Conventions in drugs field and is determined to act according to their provisions. There is a good relationship with the British Customs Administration which has assisted our department by donating modern equipment for drugs detection and provided training for the specialists performing drugs detection and analyses. Romania is also a signatory party to all UN and European Community Programmes for fighting against illegal drugs.

The Romanian Customs Administration and other authorities involved in the fight against drugs (Police, Ministry of Health etc) have been preoccupied with the harmonisation of the legislation concerning drugs, assisted by UN and European Community experts. They have drawn up drafts of law concerning the production and the legal control of chemical substances and the fight against illegal drugs trafficking.

CURRENT DRUGS POLICY AND STRATEGY IN THE SLOVAK REPUBLIC
Tana Kupkovicova, Police Officer, National Drug Service, Bratislava

In April 1994 the National Council of the Slovak Republic recommended to the Government of the Slovak Republic the institution of the National Programme to Combat Drugs and at the same time the Government was asked to establish an inter-ministerial body aimed at fighting drugs.

In August 1995 the Government accepted the proposal of the National Programme to Combat Drugs which was finalised in collaboration with the interested ministries. Simultaneously the Committee of Ministers on Drug Dependence and Drug Control was established with its General Secretariat at the Office of Government of the Slovak Republic. This has been established on behalf of our membership in international organisations and international conventions (especially UN Conventions) which were also ratified by the Slovak Republic.

The National Programme to Combat Drugs

The year 1989 represented a break not only from the point of view of social and political developments but also from the point of view of the security situation and most of all of the drug scene. In the period after 1989 there was an explosion of the number as well as the variety of crimes recorded. The opening of the borders, the liberalisation of society, the lack of legislation, the change in the value system and especially the efforts of foreign producers and distributors of drugs meant that the Slovak territory as well as some groups of inhabitants were linked to the international network of drug trafficking. Also the social and political changes in the former Soviet Union and the Balkan war influenced this situation and this was reflected in changes to the traditional smuggling routes.

Approximately 80 years' efforts to restrict drug use to medical and other licit purposes have resulted in the present international drug controls. The 1961, 1971 and 1988 UN Conventions which are also the basic platform for the drugs policy of the Slovak Republic represent a completion of this process.

In the recent past various proposals have appeared (especially abroad) recommending that the present form of drug control should be abolished or changed substantially. These proposals concerned possession of drugs for personal use. It was suggested that people should not be punished for possession of small amounts, but that commercial sale should still be a crime. Under these circumstances however, it would not be possible to judge what amount is admissible for personal consumption. Another proposal is the so called legalisation of prescriptions. Thus the existence of small dealers would be legalised and they might be utilised by drug consumers.

All the efforts of the Slovak Republic will be aimed at further drug control and reducing supply and drug demand. Strategies must be created to save young people from drugs on the basis of good co-operation among the state administration, social institutions, voluntary organisations and parents in the field of prevention, treatment and social reintegration. Combating the drug problem is not possible without close international co-operation at the global level. All isolated efforts are condemned to failure. From the point of view of prevention, the experience of other countries shows that former users can be relatively successfully treated and socially reintegrated.

The National Programme to Combat Drugs is intended to be the principal document for the activities of all the bodies of the Slovak Republic in this field. It stresses the necessity for drug control and restricts drug use for medical purposes. The objectives and strategy involve tasks for the interested ministries or other central bodies of the state administration. These tasks are either of a legislative character or they involve training and educational activities, establishment of new organisational structures and improvement of technical equipment. From a financial point of view, some tasks are possible to carry out within the current activities of the ministries, whilst some must be carried out thanks to foreign help (UNDCP, PHARE, bilateral help) or sponsorship. The prior tasks and projects of the Programme must be financed through the National Fund for drug abuse control and effective prevention, treatment and social reintegration of drug addicts.

The Committee of Ministers is a body of the Government established for specifying the strategy of combating drugs and drug dependence. Its main assignment is to initiate the programme, to develop it, to make it topical, to prepare materials for determining the major tasks of drug policy in a certain period and to evaluate the programme. The committee has been established as a superior body in order to include the entire extent of multidisciplinary drug issues whilst not interfering in the competencies of single ministries. The chairman of the Committee of Ministers is the deputy prime minister, the members of the Committee are ministers and the Attorney General. The General Secretariat has been established at the Office of the Government of the Slovak Republic. Its task is to provide organisational, administrative and technical support for the Committee.

Objectives and Strategy
A.   Prevention, treatment, rehabilitation and social reintegration
In the Slovak Republic it is necessary to pay great attention to potential as well as active addicts. Besides the repression and elimination of illicit drug trafficking, activities in the field of community prevention are needed, with a specific approach to the family, in the school and at work, in hobby activities and other spheres of social life. That is why a complex programme of measures to reduce demand for drugs must be developed.

The field of prevention can be divided into three: primary prevention includes creating the best possible conditions for the physical, psychological and social development of the individual. Secondary prevention is to prevent the existence of defects in social and psychological development, to monitor them initially and to arrange where necessary immediate measures for the individuals in danger. Tertiary prevention is to prevent deterioration of the addict's state and relapse and to minimise the consequences of drug dependence.

In the field of prevention, treatment and subsequent social reintegration we will support the ongoing opening of special facilities to serve drug addicts. These facilities will provide prophylactic and prevention activities, early diagnostics and treatment, psychological and medical help to risk groups and in addition to detoxication they will also provide rehabilitation and long term social reintegration. All the components of this care must be linked. Research will help to define the need and thus the response, on a local, regional and individual basis.

B.   Law enforcement in the fight against drugs
Illicit drug trafficking is one of the main reasons for the mass demand for drugs. That is why the illicit drug trafficking in the area of the Slovak Republic must be suppressed. The aim of suppression is to identify and paralyse criminal networks, to expose the crimes and to punish the perpetrators. The punishment of drug traffickers and dealers, but also those who help legalise proceeds or otherwise profit from illicit drug trafficking, will contribute towards the elimination of drug deliveries and distribution. The most important task is to bring the regulations which concern drug issues into accordance with the international conventions and law.

We must institute a law which will amend the use of narcotic drugs and psychotropic substances for medical and scientific purposes to provide a legal basis for prevention programmes, for general prevention, and for taking special measures against persons who are in danger of drug dependence risk and related crimes. We need controls to prevent the diversion and misuse of basic chemical substances for illicit drug production. We need to create better conditions for the sector of the state administration which is dealing with drug law enforcement, ie in the field of technical equipment and training and also on the basis of international co-operation. Special attention will be paid to the analysis of the legislation in force at present and to preparation of amendments to the Penal Law and Penal Code in line with international legislation in this field.

C.   Mass media policy
Such a policy can contribute through promoting a healthy and drug-free way of life. Counter-propaganda is also needed on the dangers of drug dependence. The main aim of a media policy is to give the facts about drugs, about the interested organisations dealing with anti-drug activities and to get the broadest possible public acquainted not only with the life of drug addicts but also with the possibilities of rehabilitation. The public need information about the various state and non-state facilities.

D.   International co-operation

As the drug problem is a common problem for all the countries in the world, it is not possible to solve it solely by national measures. Drug control and the reduction of demand for drugs requires developed international co-operation. The Slovak Republic is striving to take part in all the activities of the international community in combating drugs.

International co-operation is aimed first of all at the United Nations. Within the UN bodies it is based on 3 conventions, ie the Single Convention on Narcotic Drugs of 1961 amended by the 1972 Protocol, the Convention on Psychotropic Substances of 1971 and the UN Convention against Illicit Traffic in Narcotic Drugs and Psychotropic Substances of 1988. The Slovak Republic is obliged to introduce the conventions into the Penal Code and to co-operate with the United Nations Drug Control Programme (UNDCP) which was established as a UN body responsible for co-ordination of the international activities in the field of drugs. The member countries are also obliged to co-operate with the World Health Organisation (WHO) HONLEA etc. Co-operation within European structures is aimed at the Council of Europe, first of all at the ministerial (Pompidou) Group. This co-operation will concern health care, education, information science and repression. Co-operation with the European Union will be aimed at the co-ordination of the activities of the Slovak Republic within the European Plan to Combat Drugs. Other specialised international organisations of which the Slovak Republic is a member must be involved, ie INTERPOL (International Criminal Police Organisation), WCO (World Customs Organisation) and others.

Tasks up to 1998 and beyond

To achieve the aims of the National Programme to Combat Drugs, specific tasks for interested ministries as well as for other bodies which are responsible within their respective areas of competence for fulfilling the strategy of drugs policy have been laid down.

For the Ministry of the Interior its specific objectives are as follows:
- Building up the recently established National Drug Service as a specialised unit to combat drug abuse.
- Increasing the level of police activities in the detection and documentation of drug crimes. Improving expertise and analytic activities in co-operation with UNDCP.
- Providing regular training for police officers, also in co-operation with international organisations.
- Developing international co-operation in the field of the fight against drug abuse (especially via INTERPOL and UNDCP) as well as mutual co-operation and the exchange of experience of the ministries involved in law enforcement.
- Participation in the preparation of the law on precursors, dealing with chemical and specialised pharmaceutical production control and distribution
- Co-ordinating the activities of the Police Force and the Customs Service

Besides specific objectives for all the interested ministries (the Ministry of Health, the Ministry of Labour, Social Matters and Family, the Ministry of Education, the Ministry of Economy, the Ministry of Agriculture, the Ministry of Finance, the Ministry of Justice, the Ministry of Interior and the Attorney General's Office) joint tasks for all of them have been laid down:

They are the following:
- To propose and participate in the elaboration and preparation of legislative amendments with the aim of unifying legislation in the field of combating drug abuse, to introduce international conventions and obligations into our legal system and to approximate our legal system to the legal system of the EU.
- To build up and improve the internal information system for the collection and evaluation of data concerning drug issues.
- To establish the organisational structures to develop a more effective and qualified approach in combating drugs.

The drug scene in the Slovak Republic

The drug scene in the Slovak Republic is characterised by the intense dynamism of its development. This development began shortly after November 1989 when the Slovak Republic gradually became an important transit point on the routes at which narcotic and psychotropic substances are illegally transported. The problem of misusing drugs has been rising in parallel and a domestic market has been created by degrees. We note the growth of the number of consumers from ever younger age groups and the increase in the number of drug addicts.

The Slovak Republic is not only a transit point but also a user country especially within the context of the Balkan route. This results from the fact that new routes from the Balkans have encroached upon our territory. The principal drug transported on the Balkan route is heroin. The prevailing traffic is by land predominantly by truck. In 1995 cars and caravans started being used for trafficking, along the so called tourist routes. At the same time a new development occurred, part of the transported heroin being left for the domestic market.

The internal production of drugs, particularly cannabis, is also characteristic. On the basis of the detected cases so far it is evident that cannabis is being cultivated in almost all the areas of Slovakia. At present, however, it does not appear to involve organised groups. Cannabis producers produce cannabis mostly for their own consumption and for their friends' and acquaintances' needs. However, recently we have recorded cannabis appearing on the domestic market and it is now becoming the subject of illicit trafficking.

The Slovak Republic must also be prepared for the possibility of illegal chemical production especially with regard to the existing developed chemical industry, the continuing privatisation process and the high level of professional knowledge of potential perpetrators. Synthetic drugs are becoming an important element in the illicit drug market in the whole of Europe. They can be produced in clandestine laboratories with a minimum need for technological equipment. The resulting product is comparatively cheap and can easily be distributed. Besides the dominant drugs (heroin and cannabis) large quantities of cocaine, hashish and synthetic drugs are available.

Seizures of Drugs in 1995

The territory of the Slovak Republic is often misused by drugs dealers to avoid prosecution in their mother countries. Success in combating drug crimes is closely connected with the level of co-operation between the police units and other law enforcement bodies not only within the Ministry of Interior but also outside it. The most important partner from outside is the Customs service. In the near future we intend to establish a common workplace for the Police and Customs service. Drug crime statistics in 1995 are shown in Table No. 1

Table No. 1   Drug Crimes in 1995

criminal offences	number of cases reported cases	number of successful total	% of success (6-15)	number of prosec.persons- (15-18)	number of prosec.-children	number of prosec-minors
narcotic and psychot. sub	565	543	96.1	493	4	77
drug addict. propagation	41	41	100	39	30	6

Source: Information Service Department, Police Force Headquarters, Bratislava

According to data from the National Drug Service, the amount of drugs seized in the territory of the Slovak Republic is shown in Table 2.

In 1995 several nationals of the Slovak Republic were detained abroad. These were the people misused as couriers transporting heroin to the states of Western Europe. Table No. 3 shows the results:

In our Republic in particular, foreign nationals are involved in committing drug-related crimes. Those most involved are nationals of the former Yugoslavia (Kosovo Albanians), of Italy, of the states of the former Soviet Union and some ethnic groups (Turks and nationals of Arabian states). On the basis of family connections they create communities in the territory of the Slovak Republic and organise drug trafficking. They are equipped with the most up-to-date techniques and have a large amount of financial means at their disposal. Recently the operations of Russian and Chechen mafias have been noted. They have succeeded in gaining good links with organised groups involved in drug-related crimes.

Table No. 2   Seized Drugs in 1995

seized drugs	amount (g)
heroin	125,000
cocaine	27,150
cannabis	14,252
hashish	4,580
amphetamine	9.87

Table No. 3

detained persons	country	amount of seized drug
2	Hungary	37.8 kg of heroin
1	Switzerland	8.4 kg of heroin
2	Austria	0.043 kg of heroin
2	Italy	10.7 kg of heroin
2	Norway	10.0 kg of heroin

International Co-operation

Besides the measures within our Republic great success has been achieved at the international level. The Slovak Republic has actively contributed to the preparation of the agreement on sub-regional co-operation - the Memorandum of Understanding - and was also one of the signatory states to the Memorandum (together with the Czech Republic, Hungary, Poland and Slovenia). Within this international agreement the Slovak Republic has joined the UNDCP projects. Two in particular involve drugs control - one involves increasing operational effectiveness in the sub-region, and the other involves the training of sniffer dogs.

The international conference of ministers of the countries of the Central European Initiative responsible for combating drug abuse is to be held in the Slovak Republic in October 1996.

———————————— ● ————————————

A selection of ISTD publications

- **The ISTD Handbook of Community Programmes for Young & Juvenile Offenders.** Compiled and edited by Carol Martin. Detailed information on over 150 projects in England and Wales working with young people aged 10-21. Foreword by Barbara Mills QC. Published by Waterside Press. January 1997. 255 pp. **£13.50.** ISBN 0 901541 40 0

- **The Directory of Criminology.** The first guide to UK institutions in which criminology is taught and researched, and the courses available, together with the individuals involved and their research interests. 195pp. Published 1995. Members: **£6.50** Non-members: **£11.50.** ISBN 0 901541 34 6

OCCASIONAL PAPERS:

- **Inspectorate Independence: Desirable or Essential?** AGM 1996 Address by Sir David Ramsbotham, HM Chief Inspector of Prisons. **£1.50**

- **Eve Saville Memorial Lecture 1995 - Between Prison and Probation: the Development of Intermediate Sanctions in Western Countries.** Professor Michael Tonry, University of Minnesota. **£1.50**

- **Eve Saville Memorial Lecture 1994: The Courts & the Challenges of the Multi-Cultural Society.** Mr Justice Brooke, Chairman of the Law Commission. **£1.50**

- **Eve Saville Memorial Lecture 1993: Handling Persistent Young Offenders: Next Steps.** John Harding, Chief Probation Officer, Inner London Probation Service. **£1.50**

- **Psychopathy: A legal and clinical dilemma.** Dr John Reed. AGM 94 Address. **£1.50**

- **Understanding the Paedophile.** (published jointly with the Portman Clinic) 32pp (1989) **£3.00**

- **History of the ISTD** - David Rumney and Eve Saville. Ed. Adrian Arnold. 144pp. (1992) **£5.00**

CONFERENCE REPORTS

- **Deaths in Custody: Caring for People at Risk.**
  Ed. Alison Liebling. Published by Whiting & Birch. *Contributions from*: Sir Louis Blom-Cooper, Ian Dunbar, Lindsey Hayes, Alison Liebling, David McDonald, Gethin Morgan, Rod Morgan, David Neal, Terry Waite and selected seminar papers from the ISTD conference organised in Cambridge in 1994. Published December 1996. 226 pp. *Special price from ISTD*. **£12.00**

- **Absent from School: Truancy & Exclusion.** Eds. Carol Martin and Stephanie Hayman. A combined report from ISTD's two conferences on this theme, held in February (London) and September (Manchester) 1996. *Contributions from:* Marva Buchanan, Avril Calder, Sue Chesterton, Angela Devlin, Lorna Farrington, Liz Jones, Edwin Lewis, Nicola Mackereth, Carl Parsons, John Simkins & Patrick Younge. Published February 1997. 66 pp. **£7.00.** ISBN 0 901541 41 9

- **Child Sexual Abuse: Myth & Reality.** Ed. Stephanie Hayman. A report on the conference held at King's College London on November 25th 1996. *Papers from*: Lady Justice Butler-Sloss, Donald Campbell, Robert Hale, Barbara Kahan, Allan Levy QC, Kevin Smith, Sara Swann, Brian Waller, Norman Warner. Published February 1997. 36 pp. **£7.00.** ISBN 0 901541 42 7

- **Does Punishment Work?**
  Proceedings of a conference organised by **ISTD, The What Works Group** and **Positive Justice** in November 1995 and edited by James McGuire and Beverley Rowson.*Contributions from*: Derek Blackman, Charmian Bollinger, David Carson, Danny Clark, Andrew Coyle, David Garland, Bryan Gibson, Malcolm Gillan, Patricia Green, Leroy Logan, Doris Layton MacKenzie, Sue McCormick, James McGuire, Jerome Miller, Philip Priestley, Jenny Roberts, Michael Schluter, Joanna Shapland, Stephen Shaw, Rosemary Thomson, Martin Wasik, Dick Whitfield, Rt Hon Ann Widdecombe MP, Jean Wynne. (1996) 88pp. **£7.00.** ISBN 0 901541 39 7

- **What Works with Young Prisoners?**
  Collected papers from a conference organised by ISTD with the Trust for the Study of Adolescence at HMYOI & RC Glen Parva in November 1995. Ed. Stephanie Hayman. **Plenary Presentations:** Susan Bailey, Roger Bullock, Roger Graef, Alison Liebling **Seminar contributions:** Linda Blud, Sue Evershed, Juliet Lyon, Jane Mardon, Martin McHugh, Mary McMurran, Glen Thomas, Barbara Tudor, David Waplington, Boyd Whitehead. 52pp. **£6.00.** ISBN 0 901541 38 9

- **Managing Risk: Achieving the Possible**
  Collected papers from a conference organised by ISTD in April 1995. Eds. Julia Braggins and Carol Martin. **Plenary presentations:** Sir Louis Blom-Cooper, David Carson, Glynn Harrison, Andrew von Hirsch, Richard Lingham, Judge Christopher Pitchers, Judith Pitchers, John Reed, Baden Skitt, Graham Smith, Richard Tilt, John Wadham, Jayne Zito. **Seminar contributions:** Walter Brennan, Tom Swan, Mitch Egan, Christine Lawrie, Ruth Mann, Barry Mitchell, Herschel Prins, Roger Tarling, Hilde Tubex, 90pp. **£7.00.** ISBN 0 901541 37 0

- **Dealing with Drugs: A new philosophy?**
  Collected papers from a conference organised by ISTD in March 1995.Ed. Carol Martin. Papers by Denis O'Connor, Nicholas Dorn & Toby Seddon, John Grieve, Mike Hindson, Howard Parker & Fiona Measham and Nigel South. 40pp. **£6.00.** ISBN 0 901541 35 4

- **Serious Young Offenders: Security, Treatment & Future Prospects.**
  A report of the conference organised by the ISTD in October 1994. Eds. Ian Heritage and Carol Martin. Papers by Malcolm Stevens, Dr Sue Bailey and Professor Eugene Ostapiuk. 32pp. **£6.00.** ISBN 0 901541 33 8

- **Contracts to Punish: Private or Public?**
  Collected papers from a conference organised by ISTD in Manchester in November 1994. Ed. Carol Martin. Papers by Paul Cavadino, Robin Halward, Ken Pease, Mick Ryan and Stephen Shaw. 32pp. **£6.00.** ISBN 0 901541 36 2

- **Resolving Crime in the Community: Mediation in Criminal Justice.**
  Collected papers from a conference organised by ISTD and the London Victim-Offender Mediation Network in September 1994. Papers from John Braithwaite, Australian National University; Teresa Reynolds, Victim Support; Terry O'Connell, New South Wales Police Service. Ed. Carol Martin. 32pp. **£6.00.** ISBN 0 901541 32 X

- **Victim Offender Mediation.** A report of the conference held jointly by ISTD and Mediation UK in London in February 1994. Papers by Marian Liebmann, Eric Morrell & Philip Priestley. 20pp. **£1.50.**

- **Changing Policing: Business or Service?** A report of the Mannheim Centre/ISTD conference held in September 1993 at the London School of Economics. Ed. Carol Martin. 44pp. **£5.00.** ISBN 0 901541 30 3

- **Prison and After: What Works?** A report of ISTD's international residential conference held in Royal Holloway College in April 1993. Ed. Nic Groombridge. 56pp. **£6.00.** ISBN 0 901541 29 X

- **Values for Change: Mental Health Services in a Secure Environment.** A report of the MIND/ISTD conference held in November 1992 at King's College London. Ed. Ian Bynoe. 48pp. **£6.00.** ISBN 0 901541 31 1

CJM
Criminal Justice Matters
ISTD

CRIMINAL JUSTICE MATTERS provides information and informed opinion on all aspects of criminal justice including the police, the magistracy, crime prevention, forensic psychiatry, prisons, victims, women and crime, the law, probation and the judiciary both in Britain and abroad.

DESIGNED to be accessible and readable, CJM is essential reading for all who are concerned about crime and who want to be informed about the criminal justice process.

RECENT ARTICLES INCLUDE:
Howard Parker on the New Drug Users
Frances Heidensohn on Women in Policing
Betsy Stanko on Gender & Crime
David Garland on Surveillance and Society
Herschel Prins on Mental Disorders and Crime
Andrew Ashworth on Sentencing and Fairness
Russell Dobash et al on Steroids and Violence

Roy Porter on the History of the 'Drugs Problem'
An Interview with *James Q Wilson*
Michael Howard on the Crime Bill

FORTHCOMING ISSUES WILL FOCUS ON:
Crime and Justice in Europe
Young People in Trouble
Criminal Networks

ISTD also owns the British Journal of Criminology, published on its behalf by the Oxford University Press.

ISTD exists to promote the exchange of knowledge, experience and understanding of criminal justice. A non-campaigning body, the Institute seeks to bring together criminal justice practitioners, sentencers, policy makers and academics through a programme of conferences, courses, seminars, lectures, study visits and publications.

Please contact ISTD for further information about membership and about our publications and programme. Tel: 0171 873 2822.

The Institute for the Study and Treatment of Delinquency
King's College London, Strand, London WC2R 2LS